LIGHTNING STRIKES

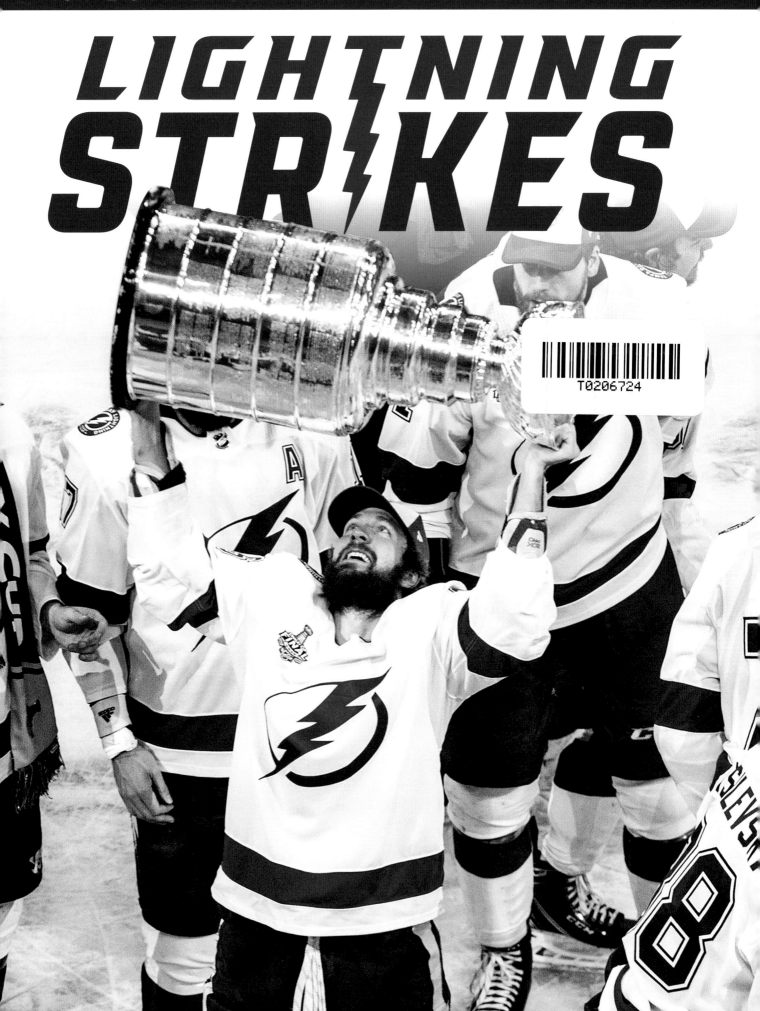

This book is available in quantity at special discounts for your group or organization.
For further information, contact:

Triumph Books LLC
814 North Franklin Street
Chicago, Illinois 60610
Phone: (312) 337-0747
www.triumphbooks.com

Printed in U.S.A.
ISBN: 978-1-62937-819-0

Content packaged by Mojo Media, Inc.
Joe Funk: Editor
Jason Hinman: Creative Director

Front and back cover photos by AP Images

All interior photos by AP Images

CONTENTS

INTRODUCTION

The road to a Stanley Cup title is a trek up a steep mountainside.

Along the way there are potential pitstops and roadblocks, patches of ice that could result in a slip up and slide back down the path. Snow drifts and a possible avalanche could end it all.

It's a treacherous marathon not meant for those who choose to bring their dancing skates.

The 2020 Stanley Cup champion Tampa Bay Lightning, however, stared up that mountain and attacked it like a grade-school student joyfully hopping around in the puddles as rain poured down from up above.

Embrace the suck and dance in the rain.

"That's the mindset that we have to bring to this whole thing and that has been our message to our players," Lightning general manager Julien BriseBois said.

One playoff season removed from a record-breaking regular season followed by an embarrassing sweep out of the postseason at the hands of the Columbus Blue Jackets, the Lightning embarked on a 2019-20 season seeking to write a different story with a better ending. Tampa Bay wanted to do that with a laser sharp focus and not let anything distract the team from the ultimate goal.

Down the stretch of the regular season, the Lightning were putting themselves in position to begin writing the final chapters in that new story before the sports world—and most of the world in general—were forced to hit the pause button due to the COVID-19 pandemic.

On March 12, 2020, Tampa Bay sat in second place in the Atlantic Division and the Eastern Conference standings and were in prime position to be considered one of the favorites to compete for the Cup.

That was followed by months of uncertainty surrounding whether hockey would be able to return, and if it was, would it be in a safe environment during a global pandemic? Would the players, who have been away from the ice for months, even be in proper shape when it did return?

Like everything else, there were no clear answers.

By June, a plan was in place to get players back to team facilities for small group workouts with the intention of putting together a return to play format.

"It's something that we've all been waiting for," defenseman Kevin Shattenkirk said when those small group workouts resumed. "But more than anything for us players, it just gives us some sense of a routine and a program to follow at least for the time being. It gives you a different set up only having six guys there

Lightning captain Steven Stamkos celebrates a long-awaited first Stanley Cup trophy.

and having to follow the protocols but it gives us the best chance to resume what we do both off the ice and on the ice while keeping ourselves protected and safe as possible."

The virus put a crimp on those plans when six members of the Lightning, including three players, tested positive for COVID-19 and shut down the team facility for several days.

But the team and the league forged ahead with the plan to begin play in early August with training camps that opened on July 13. That's when BriseBois put together the phrase that described Tampa Bay's attitude in the return to play.

Whatever happened in the past means nothing. Whatever happens during the journey doesn't matter.

It was all about maintaining full focus.

"We can't focus on the negatives," BriseBois said. "We have to turn it into positives and we just have to enjoy it and be grateful that we're getting the opportunity to compete for the Cup and write our own ending to our story."

What a story it turned out to be and in an ending unlike any other.

This championship run, spending 62 days inside the NHL bubble, first in Toronto and then on to Edmonton, played out in empty arenas filled with tarps covering the seats. Voices, normally drowned out by the roar of the crowd, echoed throughout the building.

And for Tampa Bay, they fully embraced it all. It wasn't normal, not by any stretch. There were no family members around to share moments with. There was no traveling back-and-forth. Off days were spent kicking field goals and soccer balls at nearby stadiums or tossing around a baseball or games of Spike Ball.

Tampa Bay danced through it all, putting aside any and all of the negativity that surrounded the team since falling to the Chicago Blackhawks in the 2015 Stanley Cup Final. All the disappointments of the past fueled the joy of the present.

It proved all part of a trek up redemption road, first knocking off the team that took them out the year before. Next it was the Boston Bruins, arguably the team's biggest rival the past few seasons. Then it was the New York Islanders, coached by the same Barry Trotz who was behind the bench for Washington in 2018 when Tampa Bay blew a 3-2 series lead to the Capitals in the Eastern Conference finals.

To cap it all off, it was former Lightning associate coach Rick Bowness standing in the way now calling the shots for the Dallas Stars, taking over as interim coach midway through the season.

It all gave it the feel of something that was all meant to be for a Lightning team that dealt with close calls and soul-crushing defeats.

"You need a lot of good players to get to this point and resiliency once you get to the playoffs," BriseBois said. "It really does come down to resiliency and taking advantage of the breaks that you get along the way and overcoming the breaks that go against you along the way. Ultimately, I think what it comes down to is simple, it comes down to resiliency."

The Lightning embraced it all and set up a dance with Lord Stanley unlike any other.

Let it rain. ■

Right wing Nikita Kucherov (86) and goalie Andrei Vasilevskiy (88) hoist the Stanley Cup after defeating the Dallas Stars in Game 6. The championship marks the successful conclusion to a long journey following postseason disappointment in 2019.

SEPTEMBER 19, 2020 · EDMONTON, ALBERTA
STARS 4, LIGHTNING 1

WAKE UP CALL

Lightning Enter Final Looking Less Than Fully Charged

The start of the Stanley Cup Final normally brings out plenty of energy, excitement and anticipation.

Better was expected from the Tampa Bay Lightning for their first appearance in a Cup in five years. While the Lightning did play their best in the end, with no legs and no minds to start the game, it was all for naught in a 4-1 loss to the Dallas Stars.

Now, for the second time in these playoffs, the Lightning find themselves chasing a series.

Tampa Bay entered Game 1 having played 16 playoff games in 2020, but that included the most amount of overtime in NHL playoff history at more than 185 minutes. Two of the six overtime games came just earlier in the week in the Eastern Conference final against the New York Islanders: one double-overtime loss and one overtime victory that clinched a berth in the Cup Final, the type of tight, stressful games that tax the body and mind.

That was less than 48 hours before opening the series against the Stars.

"Dallas has been the benefactor probably the last two series of Game 1 resting, and we were a benefactor last series of it," Lightning head coach Jon Cooper said. "Do I think it plays a factor? I do. I think we probably dipped our toes in the water a little bit and watched them skate around for a bit."

Not only were the Lightning slow to react to pucks, losing puck battles along the boards and missing passes on several icing calls, but they were not able to establish any sort of forecheck and made a handful of mental mistakes they had avoided for the most part throughout the playoffs.

The fatigue was noticeable both physical and mental.

"We're not using that as a crutch," defenseman Kevin Shattenkirk said. "It is what it is, it's a quick turnaround. I think it was just more of the mental aspect for us."

The first two periods were far below the standard the Lightning have set for themselves, and it had more to do with Tampa Bay than Dallas.

"I'm just disappointed in the fact that we got away from our strengths," defenseman Ryan McDonagh said. "Give them credit they're a great skating, great structured team but I think we could have played to our strengths a little bit better."

On the opening goal of the game, Zach Bogosian veered off from his defensive assignment to stand up for Brayden Point after a hit by Joel Kiviranta, but as play continued, the Lightning were out of position, allowing Roope Hintz to find defenseman Joel Hanley open between the circles at 5:40.

On the go-ahead goal in the second period, the Lightning had four players in the left circle, which

Things got physical in Game 1 of the Stanley Cup Final as the Stars took early control of the series with a 4-1 win.

allowed open space for Jamie Oleksiak to skate into and take a pass from Alexander Radulov and put a puck over Andrei Vasilevskiy off a rebound. Late in the second, the Lightning failed to close the gap on Kiviranta off the rush, allowing him an open look in the slot with 27 seconds left.

"We just made some errors," Cooper said.

Tampa Bay had 43 shot attempts and 22 shots on goal in the third period but was not able to chip into the deficit.

"I think we finally just started skating in the third period," Shattenkirk said. "After the first two we kind of waited and allowed them to bring the game to us and I think we know certainly that when we flip that and play our relentless style of hockey it makes it look like teams are sitting back. So I mean you can call it them sitting on the lead but I think at the same time we generated chances, we played our best hockey in the third and obviously not the result we wanted but certainly something that we can build on." ■

SEPTEMBER 21, 2020 · EDMONTON, ALBERTA
LIGHTNING 3, STARS 2

COOL, CALM AND COLLECTED

Lightning Show No Panic Following Game 1 Loss, Even Series at 1-1

Being able to adjust and respond to losses is a championship-quality trait. In the playoffs, no team can afford to let the snowball start to go downhill because the climb back up can often be too daunting.

It's not impossible, but any stumble makes the trek long and arduous.

Heading into Game 2 of the Stanley Cup Final against the Dallas Stars, the Lightning were looking to stop that snowball in its tracks before it started to roll and do something the 2004 Tampa Bay championship team was able to do: avoid consecutive playoff losses.

Brayden Point, Ondrej Palat and Kevin Shattenkirk each scored first period goals to lead Tampa Bay to a 3-2 victory and even up the best-of-seven series at 1-1.

Nikita Kucherov, who was targeted by the Stars early in the game, responded by setting up two power play goals in the first period as the Lightning raced out to a 3-0 lead.

Tampa Bay improved to 6-0 during the postseason in games immediately following a loss.

"We believe in our group," said defenseman Kevin Shattenkirk, whose goal at 15:16 of the first period stood as the game winner. "We know that even in Game 1 here that that wasn't our brand of hockey. I think we know that when we play that way and we play our best game it's hard for teams to win. At the end of the day if we lose a game playing our best, we can deal with that. So no one gets down in the locker room, we have great leaders in the locker room, both vocally and guys who lead by example on the ice."

One of those players is Kucherov, a player often criticized through his career for Tampa Bay, seen as a scapegoat for some of the team's recent playoff disappointments and brought about an unfair label as someone who shines in the regular season but wilts in the playoff spotlight.

But in this playoff run, Kucherov has shed that label and in some of the biggest moments for the Lightning has stepped up his play. Through 18 playoff games he registered at least one point in 13 games.

One of those pointless nights came in the first game of the Stanley Cup Final, even on 13 shot

Dallas Stars goalie Anton Khudobin is crashed into by Tampa Bay Lightning's Pat Maroon during the second period of the 3-2 Lightning win.

attempts. When the team loses, and he ends up not finding a point on the scoresheet, Kucherov often has fingers pointed in his direction.

Then he has a night like Game 2 where he had two spectacular passes to set up a pair of power play goals to help Tampa Bay snap an 0-for-15 stretch with the man advantage.

On the first power play goal Kucherov received a pass from Victor Hedman and looked off the Dallas defense with a deft pass into Brayden Point sitting in bumper position right in the soft spot in the middle of the Stars' box for a quick shot that found the near top corner at 11:23.

Dallas put Tampa Bay back on the power play less than two minutes later and this time, still set up in the right circle, Kucherov faked a one-timer and quickly put a pass through the seam to find Ondrej Palat across the ice at 14:22 for a 2-0 lead.

With his two assists, Kucherov now has 28 points in these playoffs to lead all scorers while setting a Lightning franchise playoff record, passing the mark of 26 set by Brad Richards in 2004. Kucherov is now the all-time franchise playoff leader in goals, assists, points as well as assists and points in a playoff season.

And in the six games following a Tampa Bay loss in the 2020 playoffs, Kucherov has nine points and three multi-point efforts.

That sort of production just seems to come natural to the former second-round pick, but that's not what stands out to the coaching staff.

"Everybody is going to look at the wonderful skill plays he makes," Cooper said. "But you look at his battle level, you look at when he goes in for 50-50s or 40-60s and still comes out with the puck, it's impressive. That's it for me. How hard is he working and those gritty things that guys get a lot of accolades that don't have his skill level but when you got your skill he does and he still does that, that's pretty impressive."

What was also impressive was how Tampa Bay controlled the third period while protecting the lead.

After building the 3-0 lead in the first period, the Lightning got into penalty trouble in the second period, as Dallas had five power play chances, including one that carried over from the first period, cashing in on one of them to cut the lead to 3-1.

Though Mattias Janmark would cut it to 3-2 at 5:27 of the third, getting his stick on the ice as Shattenkirk was caught in between tying up the man or taking away the passing lane away and wound up doing neither, allowing John Klingberg to find Janmark's stick for an easy tap-in.

But that was only one of five shots Tampa Bay allowed in the third period. After the Janmark goal, the Lightning did not allow a shot on goal for a stretch of 11:08 and outshot the Stars 11-2 for the rest of the period.

"One thing that this team has done is they just never put themselves in panic mode," Cooper said. "Instead of trying to protect the lead they went out there and actually kind of took it to them, and not in the sense that we were trying to score but we were completely engaged. It was really calm on the bench but it's just our attitude, they don't go through the waves of the game. There's so many emotions that occur through 60 minutes it's easy to get caught up in it." ∎

Tampa Bay left wing Yanni Gourde pins Dallas defenseman Miro Heiskanen against the boards during the tightly contested Game 2 win for the Lightning.

SEPTEMBER 23, 2020 · EDMONTON, ALBERTA
LIGHTNING 5, STARS 2

'PRETTY DAMN COOL'

Steven Stamkos Makes an Emotional Return to the Ice, Sparks Lightning to Game 3 Win

Unexpected moments of magic create legendary tales told in historical context for decades.

The Tampa Bay Lightning have created a few of those through the first 28 years in franchise history.

In Game 3 of the Stanley Cup Final, Lightning captain Steven Stamkos, absent from the lineup for 211 days, emerged from behind the scenes and right into the white-hot spotlight inside Rogers Arena.

Three shifts in, Stamkos created one of those moments that fall into the legacy category.

Unavailable throughout the playoffs after dealing with a setback from core muscle surgery in March, the captain provided an emotional boost just by being in the lineup. Just three shifts into his return, he proved to be an inspiration.

That momentous shift began at the 6:44 mark when he jumped on the ice, with Tampa Bay already up 1-0, and ended 14 seconds later when he caused an eruption of emotion that resonated from Edmonton all the way to Tampa 2,300 miles to the south.

As Stamkos moved through the neutral zone up the right-wing boards, Victor Hedman hit him in stride with a pass right to his blade. With speed up ice, Stamkos was able to avoid a hip check attempt from Esa Lindell, race in to the Dallas zone and whip a wrist shot to the top far corner to give the Lightning a 2-0 lead at the 6:58. Only one other player in NHL history made his playoff debut in the Stanley Cup Final and scored a goal—Billy Taylor Sr. with Toronto in 1940.

It was one of those magical moments that only the unscripted drama of sports can provide. The type of emotional moments that send shivers down spines and put goosebumps on the back of necks.

"It was just an amazing experience to share with my teammates," said Stamkos, who delivered his first ever Stanley Cup Final goal. "There's been a lot of hard work and different things going on behind the scenes, so just to be able to get into a game and have an impact on a game which a month ago may have

Lightning center Steven Stamkos made a dramatic return to the ice after 211 days away due to a setback from core muscle surgery, spurring Tampa Bay to a Game 3 win.

never been possible. So it was amazing to be part of a huge win for us."

As Stamkos made his way down the boards with the puck on his stick, the entire Lightning bench was on their feet in anticipation and when the puck went in, it set off a celebration as if everybody had a hand in making the moment happen.

"It was amazing," Hedman said. "You can see the reaction on the ice and on our bench. When he scored that goal and just how much he means to us as a teammate, and as a leader, and as a friend."

It was the signature moment of the 2020 playoffs and will go down as one of the top goals in franchise history.

"You want to help your team win and you have to find ways when you're not on the ice to still be part of that," Stamkos said. "I've tried to do my best in that regard but it's so painful to just sit and watch and feel like you have no part of the game. But you want to have a say and you want to contribute, so tonight was an amazing experience to get out there and help our team."

Unfortunately, Stamkos was only able to take two more shifts after scoring his goal, leaving in some discomfort after his final shift with 6:18 left in the first period.

"He only had five shifts but they were probably the most efficient five shifts you're ever going to see in the National Hockey League playoff game," head coach Jon Cooper said.

Stamkos stayed on the bench for the remainder of the period but stayed in the locker room at the start of the second period. He reemerged from the tunnel and sat on the bench, where he remained for the rest of the game, only taking a couple of twirls on the ice during media timeouts.

"I wanted to play as much as I could it's just, obviously there's an issue that I've been working through," Stamkos said. "But I was just extremely happy to be out there with these guys and have a chance to be on the bench and contribute to a win. We have a lot more hockey left in this series so we're kind of focusing on the next game."

Dallas would cut the lead in half with a shorthanded goal from Jason Dickinson at 11:19 of the first period before Tampa Bay seized control of the game with a dominant second period.

Hedman scored his 10th goal of the playoffs with a power play goal 55 seconds into the second period, Brayden Point notched his playoff leading 11th goal at 12:02 and Ondrej Palat scored his 10th of the postseason with 1:55 left to make it a 5-1 lead.

But that did not take away from the impact of the goal Stamkos scored nor tarnish what it meant to the team to have the captain not only return to the lineup but score an important goal.

"Here we are watching a player come back and then do what he did in the biggest stage at the biggest time of the year, you can't script it like that," Cooper said. "You have to marvel at it. It's pretty damn cool." ∎

Steven Stamkos (91) celebrates his long-awaited return to action with teammate Patrick Maroon (14) following a first period goal from Stamkos in the Game 3 Lightning victory.

SEPTEMBER 25, 2020 · EDMONTON, ALBERTA
LIGHTNING 5, STARS 4 (OT)

ON THE CUSP OF THE CUP

Lightning Outlast Stars in Game 4, Have Championship in Their Sights

Through all the whirlwind of elements swirling throughout Game 4 of the Stanley Cup Final, the Tampa Bay Lightning found elements of calm.

With the pressures of competing for the Cup in an already stressful environment, the Lightning waded past any of the negativity to put themselves on the brink of completing a two-month journey.

And instead of making excuses, the Lightning made plays capped off with their seventh overtime win of the playoffs on Kevin Shattenkirk's power play winner, lifting Tampa Bay to a 5-4 victory and giving the Lightning a 3-1 series lead in the Stanley Cup Final.

The Lightning rallied from behind twice, shook off a late tying goal and pushed past some controversial officiating to improve to 7-1 in overtime in the playoffs (including a shootout victory against Washington in the round robin), tied for the second most overtime victories in a playoff season.

Tampa Bay won the game off an offensive zone faceoff win by Yanni Gourde—only his third in 10

attempts in the game—back to Pat Maroon, who poked it back to Victor Hedman. As Hedman shifted to his right, Maroon headed to the front of the net before the puck was handed off to Shattenkirk. The Lightning defenseman moved down to the middle of the right circle and put a wrist shot through the legs of Dallas defenseman Jamie Oleksiak that found the lane to the far post and in at 6:34 of overtime.

Shattenkirk is the fifth different Lightning player to score in overtime during the playoffs, joining Brayden Point (2), Ondrej Palat, Anthony Cirelli and Hedman.

"It's kind of every sort of emotion you can think of," Shattenkirk said on scoring an overtime winner in the Final. "I think more than anything just how happy it makes you feel to help your team win a game. I think there are a lot of guys who had some big plays tonight and a lot of times you just look at the guy who scores the game-winning goal, but it took a lot for us to get there."

Did it ever.

Tampa Bay fell behind 2-0 in the first period on

Tampa Bay Lightning defenseman Kevin Shattenkirk is pursued by Dallas Stars center Mattias Janmark during the first period of Game 4. Shattenkirk would go on to score the game-winning goal in overtime, giving the Lightning a 3-1 series lead.

a John Klingberg goal on a rebound from his own blocked shot at 7:17 and a 2-on-1 conversion from Joe Pavelski at 18:28.

Less than a minute later, however, the Lightning cut the deficit in half on a set play where Point started to generate speed up ice from his own goal line. By the time he hit the red line, Point already had a step on Jason Dickinson and took an Ondrej Palat pass in stride for a breakaway he converted for his 12th goal of the playoffs with 32.6 seconds left on the clock.

"Shatty makes a hard pass to Pally and he put the puck right on my tape with some speed," Point said. "It's a really good pass and I can walk in and make a move there on Khudobin and luckily it went in."

After Point scored his second goal of the game, and league-leading 13th of the playoffs, on the power play—batting the puck out of the air on a broken play—the Lightning were back on even ground, digging out of the hole.

"I think when Pointer scored that goal at the end of the (first) period, that's a huge goal when you look back at that game," winger Alex Killorn said. "Who knows what would have happened if he doesn't score that goal, and he's been scoring those goals all playoffs. So we rely on the big guys to score those goals and they've been coming through."

The roller coaster started from there on out, beginning with a go-ahead goal from Dallas when Corey Perry was the first to the blue paint after Tyler Seguin swung a pass from down low, off the post then the pad of Vasilevskiy into the crease at 8:26.

Yanni Gourde pulled Tampa Bay even again with the Lightning's second power play goal of the night, taking advantage of a fortuitous bounce off the skate of Esa Lindell right to Gourde in the slot with 1:06 left in the period.

Killorn put Tampa Bay ahead for the first time in the game at 6:41 of the third period, getting a pass down low from Mikhail Sergachev to wheel around the net to the right circle and spin back to release a forehand shot to the far post for his first goal since Game 3 against Boston.

"I probably haven't scored as much as I would have liked to," Killorn said. "But when your teammates score every other night you don't really worry about those type of things, you're just worried about winning, but to get that one tonight felt really good."

The feeling didn't last long though, as Dallas pulled even again at 11:35 on a Pavelski shot banked in off the knee of Shattenkirk before back-and-forth penalty calls amplified the emotions on both sides.

With the game still tied in the final minute of regulation, Perry trailed Point up the ice and put his stick between Point's legs and gave a not-so-gentle hook that sent Point to the ice with 39 seconds left to play. But Tampa Bay was not happy that Point was called for embellishment, feeling there should have been a power play.

Off the opening faceoff in overtime, Mikhail Sergachev was whistled for holding Seguin in the Lightning zone at 37 seconds as Dallas had a 4-on-3 power play for 54 seconds. But the trio of Anthony Cirelli, Ryan McDonagh and Erik Cernak was able hold the Stars at bay, getting two clears in the first minute of the power play chance before the remainder of the power play was killed off.

At 5:10 of overtime, it was Dallas's turn to be irate at the officiating when Jaime Benn was called for tripping as he got tied up with Tyler Johnson and pulled him down from behind.

Needless to say, Dallas was not happy with the call.

"That's a hockey play. That's what I saw," Dallas coach Rick Bowness said. "It's two guys, in the playoffs, and you're going for a loose puck. And they're hooking us, and we're fighting through the hook. That's what I saw.

Lightning players celebrate the thrilling Game 4 overtime triumph over the Stars, putting them one win away from the Stanley Cup trophy.

"The players want to dictate the end of the game, and they're right. They want to play 5-on-5, and let's see what happens here. And the players are right: Let them decide the game."

Ultimately it was the players that decided the game, it just came during special teams play as the Lightning converted three chances with the man advantage while Dallas came up empty on four, including the overtime opportunity.

"We know what our goal is and we're trying to get there," Sergachev said. "It doesn't really matter if they make bad calls, we go out there and kill it. I'm thankful and happy that our guys did it tonight again, killing some penalties and killed my penalty, especially, in overtime. That was huge. So we know what we're going to do and we go out there and do it." ∎

SEPTEMBER 26, 2020 · EDMONTON, ALBERTA
STARS 3, LIGHTNING 2 (2OT)

STARSTRUCK

After Double Overtime Loss, Lightning Have Yet Another Test Ahead

For the fifth time in the 2020 playoffs the Tampa Bay Lightning stared down an opponent with the opportunity to eliminate them.

This time, however, the ultimate prize was at stake. Win this one and set off a celebration.

And, for the fifth time facing that scenario, the Lightning required overtime to try to complete the task; for the third time, the task even required multiple overtimes.

Despite putting themselves in position to come out on top and get a taste of the glory they have been chasing for a half-decade, the Lightning were unable to find the winning formula, falling 3-2 to the Dallas Stars in the second overtime on Corey Perry's goal at 9:23.

Tampa Bay still holds a 3-2 series advantage heading to Game 6 and, despite falling with a chance to win it all, the Lightning maintain the same quiet confidence that has carried them this far.

"We played well enough to win that game," Lightning head coach Jon Cooper said. "It was a team that had their back against the wall and a team we're trying to close out the series. It was a good game, we had our chances and just a couple of lost battles down low that cost us on the couple goals. We keep doing that and I'll take our chances."

Tampa Bay looked tentative to start the game, afraid to make a mistake, playing not to lose. It resulted in too many soft plays on attempted clears out of the defensive zone, feeding the Stars sustained zone time.

Eventually, it led to the opening goal of the game for Dallas when Tyler Johnson had his attempt gloved down by Jamie Oleksiak. A bounce or two later and it landed in the path of Perry who roofed a shot over the shoulder of Andrei Vasilevskiy with 2:08 left in the opening period.

From then on, Tampa Bay appeared to settle into the game, and if there were any nerves, they looked to be rid of them.

The Lightning put forth a more familiar effort in the second period, and for the rest of the game.

Ondrej Palat pulled Tampa Bay even with a power move around Esa Lindell to cut across the top of the crease and tuck the puck in the opposite side of the open net at 4:37 of the second period for his 11th goal of the playoffs.

Nikita Kucherov picked up the primary assist on the play for his 26th assist of the playoffs. Kucherov become one of only three players to ever record at least 26 assists, joining Wayne Gretzky (who did it four times) and Mario Lemieux.

Early in the third, Mikhail Sergachev fired a low-hard slap shot from the left point to put Tampa Bay on top 3:38 into the third period for the potential Cup-clinching goal.

All Tampa Bay had to do was find a way to close out the final 16 minutes of the game.

It's a daunting task, trying to hold down a team that is battling to keep its Cup hopes alive. For a good portion of the period, the Lightning were successfully

Dallas Stars right wing Corey Perry (10) scores the game-winning goal on Tampa Bay Lightning goaltender Andrei Vasilevskiy (88) during the second overtime in Game 5, tightening the series at 3-2 in Tampa Bay's favor.

controlling the play.

"You're not really thinking that way when you're in the heat of the action," Cooper said. "It's about the next shift and you're coaching and guys are playing. So there was still a little bit more time left."

The game tilted when the Lightning had the puck on their stick with an opportunity to clear, and Kevin Shattenkirk, the overtime hero from Game 4, had the follow-through on his attempt disrupted by the stick of Jamie Benn.

Seguin then got the puck back to Miro Heiskanen for a point shot that was stopped by Vasilevskiy, but Joe Pavelski established a spot at the side of the crease while engaged with Ryan McDonagh and quickly found the rebound to popped it in the net with 6:45 remaining.

The Lightning had their chances in a first overtime, controlling the play with 78-percent of the shot attempts.

Even in the second overtime the chances continued with Palat's backhand chance off a rebound and Brayden Point's tip from a Victor Hedman shot that just hit the toe of Anton Khudobin's pad. It was a short time later that the Stars ended the game on another puck near the crease.

After John Klingberg was able to walk the blue line and get a wrist shot through, Perry was alone at the top of the crease with Hedman caught up too high, allowing Perry to find the rebound with enough time to collect it and push it past Vasilevskiy at 9:23 of the second overtime.

"We got to be a little bit harder there and help Vasy out," Hedman said. "I have to get back there and make a play and they put it in. So that's the end of it. We'll look over it and it got better for next game." ∎

SEPTEMBER 28, 2020 · EDMONTON, ALBERTA
LIGHTNING 2, STARS 0

REDEMPTION

The Tampa Bay Lightning Are Stanley Cup Champions

The path toward glory provides a plethora of obstacles.

But when the journey is complete, and all the blood, sweat and tears shed along that path are finally wiped away, the sense of accomplishment in reaching the destination is made even more rewarding.

For the Tampa Bay Lightning, all of that emotion came pouring out as the final seconds ticked off the clock to close out a 2-0 victory against the Dallas Stars in Game 6 of the 2020 Stanley Cup Final, capturing the second championship in franchise history.

Brayden Point set a franchise record with his 14th goal of the playoffs, a power play goal in the first period. Blake Coleman, a trade deadline acquisition, provided the insurance in the second period, and goaltender Andrei Vasilevskiy capped it off with a 22-save shutout, his first of the playoffs.

Those were the final steps on a journey that started in 2014 when the Lightning first reached the postseason under head coach Jon Cooper and were swept out of the playoffs by Montreal. They continued to walk their path with the six-game loss to the Chicago Blackhawks in the 2015 Stanley Cup Final, losing in Game 7 of the Eastern Conference final in 2016 to the Pittsburgh Penguins and again coming up short in 2018 against the Washington Capitals.

In 2019 Tampa Bay tied an NHL record with 62 wins during the regular season, only to suffer a soul-crushing sweep from the Columbus Blue Jackets in the playoffs, putting the Lightning in the history books for the wrong reasons.

But in 2020 they put a championship run together that nobody will ever forget, in the longest, strangest season in NHL history.

"If you wear the bumps, you wear the bruises, you wear the heartache, you wear the feelings . . . you wear it on your sleeve, and it keeps you up at night," Lightning head coach Jon Cooper said. "But it also drives you and it almost becomes—the fear of losing becomes greater than the joy of winning."

There were plenty of moments in the season when

Alternate captain Victor Hedman accepts the Conn Smythe Trophy as the Lightning's most valuable player in the postseason.

it looked like the journey would never be completed or that the path itself would be cut short, denying the Lightning the chance at experiencing that joy.

After a slow start, Tampa Bay put together separate winning streaks of 10 and 11 games (the latter of which was a franchise record), and the Lightning were back in familiar territory as one of the top teams in league less than a month before the playoffs.

Everything came to a screeching halt on March 12 when the NHL shut down due to the pandemic, leaving the league in limbo on whether the season could even be completed. It wasn't until May that a plan to complete the season in two pod cities was presented. Training camps did not re-open until July, and games didn't resume until August 1 to complete a season that finally ended on September 28, 382 days after initial training camps first opened.

Sixty-four days in the bubble were capped off with Tampa Bay captain Steven Stamkos receiving the Stanley Cup at center ice inside Rogers Place in Edmonton, Alberta, with all members of the team surrounding the table to be a part of the experience.

"It's been a grind, it hasn't been easy, but it's all worth it now. We're Stanley Cup champs, and we're going to be Stanley Cup champs forever," said Lightning defenseman Victor Hedman, who was named the Conn Smythe Trophy winner as the playoffs' most valuable player. "It's going to be in history. Our grandkids can look at the Stanley Cup and see our names."

Hedman and Stamkos have been the two main cornerstones of the franchise for more than a decade, Stamkos as the first overall pick in 2008 and Hedman second overall a year later. The two most tenured players on the roster have been on the journey the longest and when it came time for Stamkos, after taking his victory lap with the Cup, to pass it on, Hedman was next in line so they could share in the moment together, exchanging a quick word before the hand-off was made.

"So many guys would do anything in the world for a chance to win a Stanley Cup," said Stamkos, who missed all but one game throughout the playoffs. "There are so many great players who

Tampa Bay Lightning's Brayden Point (21) scores against Dallas Stars goalie Anton Khudobin (35) in the first period of the series-clinching win. Point's goal was his 14th of the playoffs, a franchise record.

played this game and haven't had a chance to experience what we experienced. It was amazing to be a part of this, this whole run, it was special this year to do it in the style we did it. I think it was one of the toughest championships to win, and we found a way."

The journey to get there could have fallen apart at any point along the way. Management could have reacted differently after 2019 ended the way it did. The coaching staff could have been cleaned out and the roster overhauled.

Instead they took the road less traveled that saw minor changes, a couple of roster tweaks, a slight shift in the approach to how the team played the game, plus the trade deadline additions of Blake Coleman, Barclay Goodrow and Zach Bogosian.

The Lightning didn't alter the course, just the route.

"We lost in Chicago, that was a tough feeling. Last year against Columbus when everyone had us picked, there's been a lot of adversity," forward Alex Killorn said. "But I felt like this year was our time. You put so much into this and for it to all come together with this group of guys it just feels really good."

It was a mission fortified by what had already happened along their path.

"We were not going to be denied," Cooper said. "Our players weren't going to be denied. And we have to get up here and talk about and own what happened last year, but the players took it on the chin and I can't be happier for those guys because they deserve it. Those guys have gone through so much heartache, and to come back year, after year, after year and take our swings. And to sit here all of a sudden and be talked about as the team that was here every year and how we were seen as the team that can't get it done.

"We got it done and it wasn't without failures along the way." ■

The Tampa Bay Lightning battled through adversity never seen by an NHL champion and emerged with the second Stanley Cup in franchise history.

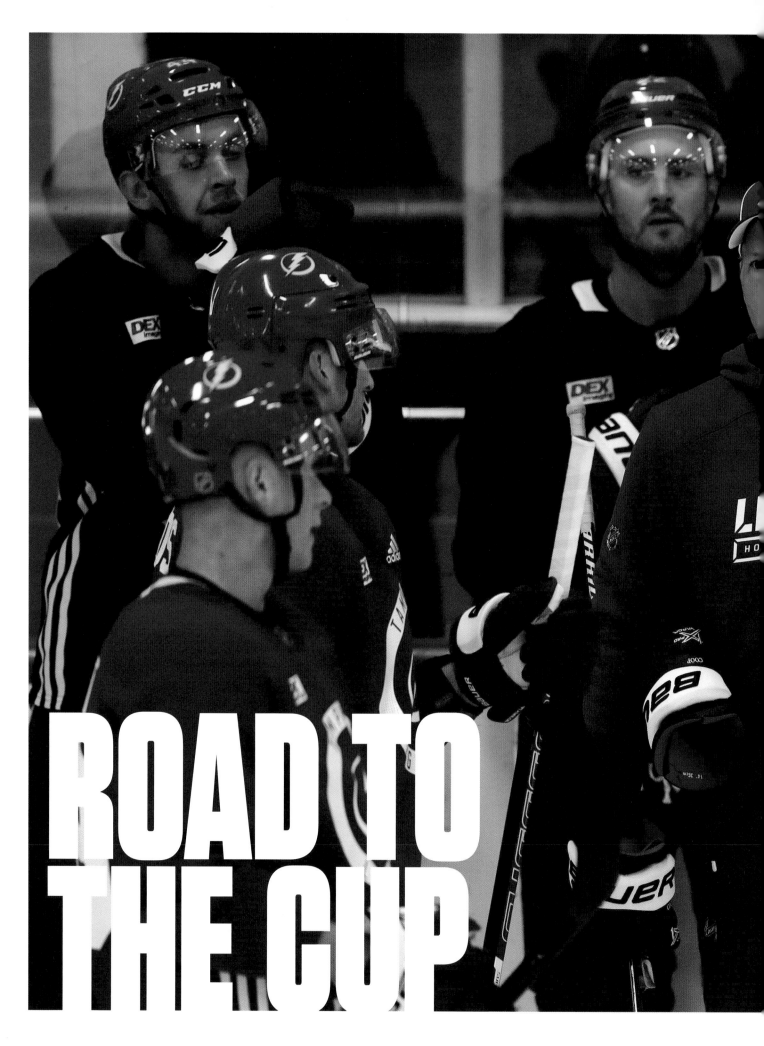

ROAD TO THE CUP

77

DEFENSEMAN

VICTOR HEDMAN

Consistency and Control Define Tampa Bay's Top Defenseman

Very few players, if any, control the game like Victor Hedman

The 6-foot-6, 225-pound defenseman defies the laws of hockey physics, gliding around the ice surface like a gazelle galloping across the savanna but doing so with the frame of a lion.

Hedman does what no other player in the game is capable of at his position.

"He is a special athlete," said Dallas Stars coach Rick Bowness, who coached Hedman for five seasons as an assistant coach with the Tampa Bay Lightning. "I've always said this about him, that I've never seen anyone 6-foot-6 skate like him. What he can do with his skating makes him such a special, special player for that size. But he's got great skills to his game, great offensive skills and that's why he's won the Norris, so that's why he's in the running every year, as he should be. He's a great player."

The No. 2 overall pick in the 2009 draft has been named a finalist for the Norris Trophy for four consecutive seasons, winning in 2018, becoming the first defensemen to earn four consecutive Norris nominations since Nicklas Lindstrom from 2005-09.

There is still more hardware in his future based on his current level of play.

After reaching the 11-goal mark in 66 games in 2019-20, Hedman has scored at least 10 goals in seven consecutive seasons and has reached at least 50 points in four consecutive seasons. He is the franchise all-time leader in goals, assists and points by a defenseman and ranks fourth all-time on the franchise scoring list. Hedman will enter the 2020-21 season needing 27 points to reach the 500-point plateau, something only 70 defensemen in NHL history have accomplished.

Those are the numbers that stand out, but it's his overall game that makes him stand out among his peers.

In the playoffs, Hedman took his game to a new level and nearly matched his regular season goal total, putting up postseason goal production in the company of some of the great defensemen in the game, including Bobby Orr, Denis Potvin, Brian Leetch and Paul Coffey.

"I think Victor Hedman has been phenomenal on the back end for Tampa Bay," former NHL

Victor Hedman was drafted No. 2 overall in the 2009 draft and has lived up to the hype as one of the best defensemen in the league during his career.

goaltender and NBC analyst Brian Boucher said. "We all know that he can skate. We all know that he can defend. He's got a great stick. He truly is—he's a superstar. Obviously, a Norris candidate. But I think he's played exceptional."

Hedman logs big minutes without ever seeming to wear down while playing in all situations. In the five-overtime marathon game to open the playoffs against Columbus, the big Swede logged more than 57 minutes of ice time, nearly the equivalent of three games worth of playing time.

His presence, his contributions do not go unnoticed by those who play alongside him.

"He's just so relentless in his play, it's very inspiring in that nature," veteran defenseman Ryan McDonagh said. "For a guy with his size and his ability, he gets up and down the ice so well and it's nonstop. As a defenseman we see that and then try to instill that in your game little bits and pieces but the way he consistently does it is impressive."

To a player like Mikhail Sergachev, who was the sixth overall pick by the Montreal Canadiens in 2016 before joining Tampa Bay via trade, Hedman is an inspiration to emulate.

"He controls the game, he plays all situations," Sergachev said. "Not only does he eat minutes, he's just so great at killing penalties, power play, at 5-on-5. It's just unbelievable how well he plays; sometimes he can play 30 minutes and do it like it's nothing and he's doing everything for us."

That includes taking charge from the leadership role that has evolved throughout his career, all of it

with the Lightning. Hedman is the second longest tenured player on the roster behind only captain Steven Stamkos, who was drafted one year prior to Hedman.

"He's been a huge leader the last few years as I've gotten to know him," said McDonagh, who joined Tampa Bay at the trade deadline in 2018. "He takes so much pride in wearing that Lightning uniform, wore it his whole career and not every player gets to do that their whole careers. He's been through a lot of ups and downs. You can see that in his play and the way he talks to our group. I think there is nobody hungrier than him and we're all just following his lead."

Hedman's play is the epitome of the strong individual benefiting the collective group.

"It's tough to say he's not the best defenseman in the NHL right now when you look at the way he's playing," Lightning forward Alex Killorn said. "He scores huge goals for us in situations where a lot of times we're down a goal, he helps us out in that sense where he gets us back in a lot of games but by an individual effort." ◼

Victor Hedman takes out Boston Bruins left wing Nick Ritchie during the third period of a 3-2 Lightning win. Hedman's versatility on the ice is admired by teammates and opponents alike.

DYNAMIC DUO

Brayden Point and Nikita Kucherov Put Forth
Supercharged Playoff Performances

Throughout NHL playoff history, plenty of high scoring, dynamic duos have put their stamp on successful runs to the Stanley Cup.

Wayne Gretzky and Jari Kurri.

Mike Bossy and Bryan Trottier.

Mario Lemieux and Jaromir Jagr.

Sidney Crosby and Evgeni Malkin.

Jonathan Toews and Patrick Kane.

Add Brayden Point and Nikita Kucherov to that conversation as the duo became the eighth pair of teammates in NHL playoff history to each record 30-or-more points in a playoff season and the first since Malkin and Crosby in 2009.

The top two leading scorers in the postseason accounted for roughly 25-percent of the team's total goals in the playoffs, and that's with Point missing two games in the Eastern Conference finals.

Point, who underwent hip surgery in the offseason, utilized the four-month pause to regain the strength in in those areas, and it showed in his skating. He made an immediate impact by scoring the winning goal in the marathon overtime game to open the first round against the Columbus Blue Jackets, putting a wrist shot from the top of the circles past Joonas Korpisalo at 10:33 of the fifth overtime. Point had the winner to clinch the opening series, also in overtime.

Point became the sixth player in Lightning franchise playoff history to record 10-or-more goals in a single postseason.

"I'd go as far as to say he's the most dangerous guy in the playoffs this year," Blake Coleman said of Point. "He's a special talent and you see that every time he's out there. Anytime you have a guy like that in your lineup you have a better chance of winning hockey games."

With Steven Stamkos absent due to injury, Point's presence took on a higher profile on the top line, and he grabbed it with full force. His goal to open the Eastern Conference final less than two minutes into the first period showed his command of his game and the tone he's capable of setting with his speed.

"He's played in some big moments in his career, given some big assignments," Lightning head coach Jon Cooper said. "I look back in 2018 when we made our run to the conference final. He was a big reason we beat the Boston Bruins and I thought that was kind of his coming out party. Injuries

Brayden Point benefited from the four-month pause of the season, as it gave him extra time to recover from offseason hip surgery, paying dividends throughout the postseason run.

probably set him back a little bit and the pause probably helped him get healthy. But he's really getting command of his game and when you play the right way I just, I truly believe good things will happen to you and that's what that kid does."

Kucherov, who is the only player in franchise history to record two 10-goal postseasons, broke six franchise records during the postseason, setting the all-time playoff mark for goals, assists and points and the single-playoff season record for points and assists.

In a postseason full of redemption for the Lightning, Kucherov was spectacular. This comes a season after finishing with 128 points in the regular season and earning an MVP trophy, only to finish with two assists, no goals and earning a one-game suspension in the first-round series against Columbus.

Kucherov took on more responsibility this time around and showed maturity as he was consistently targeted by opponents throughout the postseason.

"The attention he gets is unparalleled and you're getting that attention for a reason, it's because you are pretty darn good," Lightning head coach Jon Cooper said. "But you can't let somebody see you sweat. They're going to make it tough on you, and you just have to fight through it. The one thing is, respect is earned and it's gained when you fight through stuff. He has and he's found a way to keep his emotions in check. He's getting rewarded on the point side of things because he's sticking to his guns and he's playing to the structure, he's playing to the system. It's a lot of fun to watch."

Cooper noted how the points piled up for Kucherov, and those are the end results. But Cooper looks for other areas to see how engaged the 2019 league MVP is during games.

"Everybody is going to look at the wonderful skill plays he makes," Cooper said. "But you look at his battle level, you look at when he goes in for 50-50 or 40-60 (pucks) and still comes out with the puck, it's impressive. That's it for me. How hard is he working and those gritty things that guys get a lot of accolades that don't have his skill level. But when you got the skill he does and he still does that, that's pretty impressive."

The performance of the two together proved beyond impressive and put the pair on the list of some of the greatest displays by a duo in postseason history. ∎

Nikita Kucherov bounced back after a disappointing postseason performance in 2019 to help lead the charge to 2020 Stanley Cup glory for the Lightning.

HEAD COACH

JON COOPER

From the Courtroom to the Cup, Cooper Found Success on His Own Terms

Jon Cooper walked an unconventional path to reach the ranks of Stanley Cup-winning coaches.

He played college lacrosse at Hofstra University in New York (across the street from Nassau Coliseum, home of the New York Islanders), attended Thomas M. Cooley School of Law in Lansing, Mich. and then began practicing law.

But when he was approached to oversee a local high school hockey team, the course of his career started to slowly shift away from his law practice toward coaching, first in the youth ranks and then in junior, where he took over for the Texarkana Bandits of the North American Hockey League in 2003. After the franchise moved to St. Louis, Cooper led the team to a pair of championships in 2007 and 2008. Next was a move North to the Green Bay Gamblers of the United States Hockey League, where he collected another title in 2010.

The professional ranks came calling when he was hired by the Tampa Bay Lightning to coach the Norfolk Admirals, their American Hockey League affiliate, for the 2010-11 season. A year later, Cooper led the Admirals to a 29-game winning streak and a Calder Cup championship.

The Lightning elevated him to coach in Tampa Bay at the end of the 2012-13 season, and two years later, the franchise appeared in the Stanley Cup Final for the second time in franchise history, losing in six games to the dynastic Chicago Blackhawks.

Success seemed to come easy for Cooper at every stop along the way.

But after taking five years to return to the Final, it's apparent how much growth was required for Cooper to see his name engraved on the Stanley Cup.

"Playoffs, it's a marathon and you've just got to learn to keep your emotions in check," Cooper said. "And more importantly keep your players' emotions in check and honestly not to over-coach. And if you're doing that and you're relying on all the things that you've done to build up to this point, we're really happy with what we've done and the confidence and that. And then it's as a coach having confidence in what you've done. It's controlling those emotions, (that) is probably what I've learned I guess the most."

Tampa Bay has had its share of success under Cooper's guidance, with four Eastern Conference finals in the span of six years. But the route to

Jon Cooper took an unconventional route to become head coach of the Lightning but his success at all levels foreshadowed what he'd accomplish in Tampa Bay.

reaching the final goal took that sort of understanding and guidance after being humbled on a few occasions.

It allowed the team to grow along with their head coach. While there are still several players who have been a part of this entire run of success that started with a playoff berth in 2014, others have come in and seen the difference that Cooper makes.

"He's a phenomenal coach," said center Barclay Goodrow, who was acquired at the trade deadline. "You can kind of see why the team has had so much success of the past few years from the coaching, management and the group of guys we have. It's a special group, so it's no wonder why they have had some success."

Veteran forward Pat Maroon, who won a Stanley Cup title with the St. Louis Blues in 2019, signed a one-year deal as a free agent with the Lightning this season in part because of the chance to win back-to-back Cups, but also to reunite with Cooper.

As a teenager, Maroon played under Cooper as a member of the Bandits, first in Texarkana and remaining with the team the next season where he was the leading scorer on the road to a title.

The reunion has seen changes in both, for the better.

"I was still a young kid so obviously we have both grown as individuals," Maroon said. "He does a really good job of handling guys and managing the game and managing the players. It's been fun to watch. He's had one heckuva career as an NHL coach. He's done a great job of just being himself and kind of being that players' coach. He handles situations really good. It's been good to be back with him."

The lawyer who once spent his time in the courtroom arguing cases has now made a convincing case for his own legacy. Jon Cooper has joined the ranks of the top coaches in the game, and with this Tampa Bay Lightning team, his name is forever etched in hockey history. ■

Jon Cooper's days of practicing law are far behind him now that he has a Stanley Cup on his résumé.

'DAMNED IF I DO'

Aggressive Trade Deadline Moves Pay Off for BriseBois and Tampa Bay

During the midseason scouting meetings the Tampa Bay Lightning held in January, general manager Julien BriseBois and the staff identified what they felt would make the Lightning a harder team to play against.

The consensus focused on adding two forwards "that would be able to play a heavy, hard, competitive game," BriseBois said.

With that path mapped out, BriseBois and the pro scouting department zeroed on the two players that best fit what they were looking for: Blake Coleman and Barclay Goodrow.

BriseBois went into the trade deadline with an aggressive buyer's approach and acquired both players, while also landing defenseman Zach Bogosian as a free agent.

All three made significant impacts on the team.

"Ultimately at the deadline when you're a buyer, you're damned if you do and damned if you don't," BriseBois said. "I decided I was going to take the risk of being damned if I did."

After not making any moves at the deadline in 2019 and being unceremoniously swept out of the first round, BriseBois felt he owed it to the team to do everything possible to bring in help for the postseason without taking away from the current roster.

With the addition of Coleman and Goodrow along with the signing of Bogosian, BriseBois felt the Lightning were in the best possible position to compete for a Stanley Cup, even at the cost of two first-round picks in the 2020 draft and 2019 first-round pick Nolan Foote.

"I was in the buyer's chair and my mindset was not about value maximization, it's about winning hockey games," BriseBois said. "And I look at our team with Blake Coleman and Barclay Goodrow in there and we're a better team now, and we're going to be a harder team to take out during (the playoffs) with the addition of these two players."

Coleman, a 20-goal scorer with the New Jersey Devils, provides the type of energy and commitment the Lightning look for in their players. He added another element to a roster that BriseBois wanted to be hard to play against.

"I like our team, I believe in this group, and now I think we're just all the more stronger because we've added Blake Coleman," BriseBois said. "Not only will he make us a better, more competitive team this year, but he'll also make us a better, more competitive team next year as well.

"At this time of year (prices) were very high [but] to acquire good players you have to pay a hefty

Blake Coleman (20) was a terrific trade deadline acquisition for the Lightning for the short- and long-term outlook of the team.

premium, and we certainly did that today. But we could afford to do so. What I felt we could not afford to do is (not) give this group of players every chance to have as good a (playoffs) as possible."

Goodrow brought a physical style of game to the ice with a grinder mentality.

"We needed a big, physical center and he brings that," BriseBois said. "He has the size, he also has the physicality and he plays with an edge. Because of injuries in San Jose he was asked to play a bigger role with more skilled players and he's handled that well."

BriseBois also feels that, just like Coleman, Goodrow is at a point in his career where he's ascending.

The Lightning were additionally in position to acquire former No. 3 overall pick Zach Bogosian, a right-hand shot defenseman, after his contract was terminated by the Buffalo Sabres just before the trade deadline, making him an unrestricted free agent. Bogosian was signed to a one-year, prorated deal.

"All of a sudden he became an option for us," BriseBois said. "He wanted to be in an environment where he had a chance to win a Stanley Cup. We're a contender and with him we're a better team. He's another guy that brings us some physicality and size on the back end."

All three late-season acquisitions made their presence felt at various points of the playoffs.

Coleman scored timely goals, including one 15 seconds after falling behind in Game 4 of the Eastern Conference finals. Goodrow set up the series-clinching goal for Anthony Cirelli in Game 6 of the Eastern Conference finals. And Bogosian had the assist of the playoffs on his forward-falling pass to Coleman in Game 2 of the second round against Boston.

They all had the opportunity to fit in seamlessly, aided in many ways by team chats during the four-month pause and then the two-week summer reboot camp before the playoffs began.

"We knew them as players, we had good intel on how they were as people and they've been incredible for us, they've made us better and that was the whole point," BriseBois said. "Ultimately when you're trying to put all the pieces of the puzzle together you're accumulating talent but you're really building a team, and they were all key pieces in helping this picture kind of come together for us this year." ∎

Another key deadline addition, Barclay Goodrow (19) has added a needed level of physicality at the center position for the Lightning.

91

CENTER

STEVEN STAMKOS

On the Ice or Behind the Scenes, Stamkos Remains the Lightning Leader

Even before Steven Stamkos was selected by the Tampa Bay Lightning with the first overall pick in 2008, he served as the face of the franchise.

Not long after Tampa Bay won the draft lottery and the right to make the first selection, a marketing campaign popped up around town asking if anybody had "Seen Stamkos" with bumper stickers and billboards all over town plus a dedicated web site for the campaign that pushed the slogan around North America.

Before team management stepped to the podium in Ottawa to announce his name at the draft, Stamkos was a household name for hockey fans in Florida.

The longest-tenured player on the Lightning roster has experienced everything imaginable during his 12 years with the franchise, and some unimaginable things as well.

For the Lightning's 2020 playoff run, he found himself unfit to play after underdoing core muscle surgery on March 2, dealing with issues during rehab in June that limited him during July training camp, and finally being forced to stop practicing altogether shortly after the team arrived in Toronto on July 26.

As the team marched their way through the playoffs, Stamkos remained primarily in the background until late in the third round. The team was able to continue finding ways to win, reaching the Stanley Cup Final for the second time in five years.

"It really does come down to resiliency," Lightning general manager Julien BriseBois said about how the team found playoff success without the captain. It's about "taking advantage of the breaks that you get along the way and overcoming the breaks that go against you along the way. So ultimately, I think that's what it comes down to. Once you have a good enough team to get into the playoffs, it's who's going to find a way."

Even while remaining out of the lineup, Stamkos remained a big part of the journey for the Lightning, working behind the scenes as a leader. And when Tampa Bay captured the Eastern Conference championship, he donned his jersey and joined alternate captains Victor Hedman, Alex Killorn and Ryan McDonagh to accept the Price of Wales Trophy, sporting his best playoff beard.

"Stammer's a huge part of our team, he's our captain, he's been our captain for almost every day

Steven Stamkos missed much of the Lighting's return to hockey following core muscle surgery, but he's remained a leader and important part of the team even when not on the ice.

that I've coached," Lightning head coach Jon Cooper said. "He's a big reason why we're here and this season he hasn't played in the postseason but was a big reason we made the playoffs and he's a big reason we finished pretty high in the conference. And what I loved most about it was how the three assistant captains were going up there, but they wanted to make sure Stammer was a part of it, and he deserves to be a part of it. That's probably why you get the position that we're in right now, is because everybody cares so much for each other and we want to make sure he was in that picture."

Through his career Stamkos has had to deal with injuries that have cost him significant playing time, starting with a broken leg suffered on Nov. 11, 2013 that cost him four months and a spot on the Canadian Olympic team. At the end of the 2015-16 season he had a blood clot near his collarbone that prompted surgery to remove his uppermost rib and required him to take blood thinners, which kept him out for all but Game 7 of the Eastern Conference finals.

In November of 2016 he needed surgery to repair a partially torn meniscus in his knee, which kept him out for the remainder of the regular season when Tampa Bay missed out on the playoffs by one point.

After being healthy for the next two seasons, there was the core muscle surgery on March 2 that, under normal circumstances, would have ruled him out of the first round of the playoffs.

It's what made his absence for the 2020 playoff bubble tournament that much more difficult, since the pause was expected to benefit his rehab.

But it didn't take away from what it meant to have the captain along for the ride.

"He's the leader of this team," Hedman said. "He is such a good influence in the room during practices and morning skates so he's still a big reason that we're here where we are." ∎

Steven Stamkos (91) has fought through injuries his entire career and it ultimately paid off with a Stanley Cup championship in his 12th season as the face of the Lightning franchise.

71
CENTER

ANTHONY CIRELLI

Cirelli Makes His Presence Felt with Big Goals at Big Moments

The Stanley Cup playoffs provide a platform for players normally out of the spotlight to step directly onto center stage.

Ruslan Fedotenko, with his two goals scored for the Lightning in Game 7 of the 2004 Stanley Cup Final, serves as a prime example. In the franchise's second Cup-winning season, Anthony Cirelli showed a similar innate ability to score big goals at big moments.

Along Tampa Bay's playoff run this year, Cirelli's offensive production didn't register so much for quantity, but it offered plenty in terms of quality.

The biggest of those quality moments came in Game 6 of the Eastern Conference finals when he scored at 13:18 of overtime to capture the Eastern Conference championship and send the Lightning to the Stanley Cup Final for the third time in franchise history.

Cirelli also had an extra attacker goal in Game 5 against Columbus in the first round that pushed the game to overtime before Tampa Bay won it to advance to the second round. And then he had a third-period, go-ahead goal in Game 5 against Boston, which the Lightning eventually won in double-overtime to clinch the series and move on to the Eastern Conference finals.

Players who have a knack for seizing these moments generally also have a certain determined quality on display each time they step on the ice, something Cirelli shows particularly in his puck pursuit. It's the type of determination that makes him such an effective forechecker, just as he was on that series-clinching goal against the Islanders.

"He is persistent," Lightning defenseman Kevin Shattenkirk said. "A lot of guys on this team are great forecheckers but Anthony is someone who is so strong in his triangle and the balance on his skates, and he's so strong on his stick that he can fight off two or three guys and get the puck to other guys on his line then things happen from there. This guy is really a bright, young star and I've enjoyed watching him all year."

Stardom is not something Cirelli seeks. His role as a match-up center, which earned him a fourth-place

Anthony Cirelli carries the puck against the Florida Panthers in October 2019. A third-round selection in the 2015 draft, Cirelli has emerged as a key player in big moments for Tampa Bay.

finish for the Selke Award as the top defensive forward this season, is not generally one that claims the spotlight.

Yet, the spotlight seems to find him. Cirelli's penchant for key moments is a quality he built something of a reputation on before even reaching the National Hockey League.

As a 16-year-old, Cirelli went undrafted into junior hockey and earned a spot as a walk-on for the Oshawa Generals in the Ontario Hockey League. As a rookie, Cirelli scored both goals in the 2015 Memorial Cup championship game against Kelowna, including the overtime winner at 1:28 in the extra period.

Tampa Bay selected Cirelli in the third round of the 2015 draft before he was dealt to Erie in 2017, where he scored the overtime series-clinching goal in the OHL championship game to send Erie to the Memorial Cup.

Ask him about any of that, however, and he deflects all praise directed toward him, instead talking about his linemates and teammates. Even on the series-clinching goal against the Islanders, where Cirelli's line won the puck on a one-man forecheck surrounded by four New York players that allowed the play to develop, the man who scored the goal never even mentioned it when asked.

"That was a helluva play by Goody (Barclay Goodrow) to fake the backhand and get it to me," Cirelli said.

As he continued to answer questions regarding his emotions, he used the words "we" and "our" when describing what it means to advance to the Stanley Cup Final.

Cirelli plays with so much heart, there is no room for ego.

"Being with this group, we worked all year for this," Cirelli said. "This is our goal, is to get here . . . with a great group of guys and coaching staff and management, all the way up. I think it is exciting times." ■

Anthony Cirelli is known for his puck pursuit, shown here with Vegas Golden Knights right wing Reilly Smith defending.

88
GOALIE

ANDREI VASILEVSKIY

Vasilevskiy Stands Tall, Bounces Back in 2020 Playoffs

On a roster filled with All-Star talent and multiple trophy winners, Andrei Vasilevskiy stands in the background serving as the Tampa Bay Lightning backbone.

In just his third year as a full-time starter, Vasilevskiy provides the kind of stability in net that any championship-caliber team needs to be successful. And though he owns some hardware of his own, the 26-year-old quietly does his work without garnering many of the headlines from some of the team's more high-profile players.

"The rock of our team is for sure Vasy back there," alternate captain Ryan McDonagh said. "We just feed off that."

Vasilevskiy goes about his business of stopping pucks and picking up wins and has come a long way since he was thrust into the 2015 Stanley Cup Final, starting Game 3 in Chicago when Ben Bishop was unable to play, and then starting the final six games of the 2016 Eastern Conference finals when Bishop was injured in the opening game of the series against Pittsburgh.

Like most of his teammates, Vasilevskiy was able to grow and learn through all the playoff experiences over the past handful of years, particularly following the 2019 postseason, when the Lightning were swept out of the first round by Columbus after a record-setting regular season.

"I knew I had to stop the puck more this year," Vasilevskiy said.

While the former 19th overall pick in the 2012 draft continues to downplay his play, the growth in his game and maturity in his play is quite noticeable over the past few seasons since he assumed the starter role at the end of 2016-17.

"I think he's continued to mature," NBC analyst and former NHL goaltender Brian Boucher said. "I think you've got to go through some experiences in order to improve. Obviously he took a punch in the gut last year getting swept in Columbus, and the regular seasons were great and all that's fine. We all know that.

"But the true test comes playoff time, and when you have the pause and then you have to restart and

Andrei Vasilevskiy celebrates the team's overtime win over the New York Islanders in Game 6 of the Eastern Conference finals. Vasilevskiy allowed only one goal on 27 shots.

then face the team that knocked you out the year prior and get through it, to me, that's how you grow as a goaltender."

For Boucher, he sees Vasilevskiy forging all the elements of his game to becoming one of the top goaltenders in the league approaching the peak section of his career. Vasilevskiy has already won a Vezina Trophy as the top goaltender in the league, which he captured in 2019, and has been named a finalist for three consecutive years, his first three seasons as a full-time starter.

"A ton of talent. Obviously we know his physical ability. He's big, he's agile, he's flexible, powerful, all of the athletic qualities that you want in a goaltender," Boucher said. "I just see a much more mature goaltender now, that we knew had physical abilities and all the talent in the world, starting to put it all together now."

In the 2020 playoffs Vasilevskiy proved the model of consistency, starting every game for the Lightning and keeping his team in every single game, posting Conn Smythe-caliber numbers along the way. Through the first three rounds of the playoffs, he allowed more than three goals on only two occasions, still winning one of them. In the series against Columbus last season, Vasilevskiy allowed 15 goals in the four-game sweep.

In a bounce back postseason performance a year later, he has stood tall through it all.

"You just have guys that on every single night somebody comes to the forefront. The one difference with the goaltender is he has to be there every single night," Lightning head coach Jon Cooper said. "They probably get taken for granted a little bit, especially when you have one. But he's not overlooked in our locker room. Everybody knows the value he brings to our team." ■

Andrei Vasilevskiy learned from a disappointing 2019 postseason and used that experience to help propel the Lightning to the 2020 Stanley Cup.

THE DISTANT THUNDER ARE HEARD ALL THE WAY UP IN TORONTO

Lightning Get Creative with Fandom During a Pandemic, Bring Fans Along for the Ride

Tampa Bay's hockey club enjoys a special relationship with a very passionate fan base. They are the Lightning. The fans are the Thunder.

But after the NHL went on pause on March 12, 2020, due to the pandemic, everything changed and social distancing became the new normal, preventing the gathering of large crowds.

When the National Hockey League put together a plan to return to action with an unprecedented 24-team Stanley Cup tournament to crown a champion for the 2020 season, fans were not allowed to be a part of the experience, at least in person. The league dispatched the teams to two bubble cities—12 Eastern Conference teams went to Toronto, Ontario, and the other 12 Western Conference teams gathered in Edmonton, Alberta.

All games would be played inside empty arenas. No roar of the crowd, no thumping in the stands, none of the edge-of-your-seat moments of anticipation resulting in explosions of emotion or hushed tones of disappointment.

"It's obviously different, there are no fans in the building," center Brayden Point said after the team's exhibition game against the Florida Panthers on July 29 inside Scotiabank Arena in Toronto.

With the Lightning unable to share the playoff journey with their fans, they brought the fans with them with a campaign the team called Distant Thunder, encouraging fans to still be a part of the experience even without being there.

One unique aspect of the campaign that was revealed for that first game was a special piece of glass that was inserted into the boards in Toronto.

Before the team left Tampa, fans were invited to come to Amalie Arena during training camp and, while maintaining social distancing outside on the plaza, offer messages of support on a pane of glass that

Nikita Kucherov looks at the pane of glass that Lightning fans signed as part of the Distant Thunder fan campaign before playing against the Florida Panthers in an exhibition game ahead of the Stanley Cup playoffs in Toronto.

would travel with the team to Toronto, bringing the fans with them—virtually—for the playoff journey.

"We saw them putting it in and you know I think that's a nice touch, something that's pretty cool," Point said. "The fans put those messages out there for us . . . just awesome to have that support."

The signed glass remained with the team through three round robin games and each of the first two rounds of the playoffs, series wins against Columbus and Boston. It was something during moments of reflection the players could look over at and be reminded of the support from back home.

"You realize how proud our fans are to be Lightning fans," defenseman Kevin Shattenkirk said. "I think there's this kind of chip on their shoulder to show the world that hockey is alive and well in Florida. I think as players, you take that on, as well. The community involvement, the interaction that we have with them on a daily basis, the way that they show up to our practices—all these little things, they make you proud to put on the jersey and make you realize that you're representing not just yourself as a player or an organization but you have a few extra tens of thousands that are watching, that are working for the same goal and hoping for the same goal that you are."

When the team departed Toronto after the series victory against Edmonton, the glass was not able to travel with them because it did not fit in the board system at Rogers Place.

So instead of that glass, the team had two panes of smaller glass, with signed messages from fans, with them at the team hotel on display on the teams designated floor. In addition, there are pieces of canvas art with messages from fans on display all around the hotel, in the team's meal room and activity room along with digital displays that are shown in the building and at various points.

Five-year Lightning season ticket member Stephanie Llanes was one of those fans who took part in the project, her message prominently displayed during the team's marketing campaign.

"The glass singing was a unique experience," Llanes said. "It was a very cool way for the team to try and keep the fans involved in such a challenging time during Covid-19. It made me feel so proud to know that it would go with guys to Toronto and then Edmonton, hoping it would give them inspiration knowing the fans were behind them. I was super excited when I saw the commercial and saw my message right in the middle of the glass. Every time I see it gives me chills. I am thankful the team and the organization wanted to include fans with this opportunity."

Even though the fans were not allowed to be there in person, they were with them at almost every step along the most unusual journey to a Stanley Cup.

"It's just it's like bringing a little piece of home with us," Lightning head coach Jon Cooper said. "It just makes you . . . you don't feel like we are by ourselves here. We got that feel that everyone is behind us." ■

Alex Killorn skates by the signed glass, a gesture by the organization which resonated with players and fans alike.

PLAYOFFS

An "End Racism" message is displayed before Game 3 of the second-round matchup between the Lightning and the Bruins. The campaign is part of an anti-racism initiative in partnership with the recently player-formed Hockey Diversity Alliance.

AUGUST 3, 2020 • TORONTO, ONTARIO
LIGHTNING 3, CAPITALS 2

NUTS AND BOLTS

Lightning Return to Play with Hard-Fought Win Over Capitals

In the first real action in nearly five months, the Tampa Bay Lightning needed to regain the feel of the game once again.

Andrei Vasilevskiy stopped 31 shots, Nikita Kucherov scored a goal and added the shootout deciding marker and Mitchell Stephens notched what officially is his first career playoff game in a 3-2 victory for Tampa Bay against the Washington Capitals.

But this wasn't a true playoff game; it was a round-robin game to determine the top four seeds ahead of the Conference Quarterfinals next week.

It did, however, evolve into what felt like a playoff game. And that was just what the Lightning needed before the start of the first round.

Tampa Bay had a relatively easy go of things in their only other game played since coming back, a 5-0 exhibition victory against the Florida Panthers. That was hardly a test, more of a 10-question, multiple-choice, open-book math quiz.

The one numerical figure needed to discern the difference between that game and the match-up against Washington showed in the hit column. In the game against Florida the two teams combined for 48 hits. Against the Capitals, the Lightning alone registered 45 while the teams combined for 89.

"I think anytime you can start mimicking any sort of playoff game, with the energy and physicality,

it's good for your team," Lightning head coach Jon Cooper said. "I wasn't sure how these three (round-robin) games were going to go. We get into one that was close and competitive, it went overtime, we had to kill off a four-on-three chance, different situations in the game. I think we did a really good job."

Tampa Bay built a 2-0 lead on an all-world shot from Nikita Kucherov and a net-front deflection from Stephens.

That's about the time the Capitals started to change their tactics with some not so subtle plays to try and get the Lightning to engage. Witness Garnet Hathaway delivering a late hit from behind at center ice to Cedric Paquette. Or T.J. Oshie giving Yanni Gourde a punch to the back of the head while the two were going up ice. Or Tom Wilson delivering a couple of jabs to Anthony Cirelli during a scrum behind the net while being held by a linesman.

Tampa Bay's lead disappeared in the span of two minutes and eight seconds on goals from Richard Panik and Evgeny Kuznetsov, the latter coming on a power play.

The lead may have disappeared, but Tampa Bay didn't.

"We pushed for 35 minutes and then in the second period there we kind of lost our cool, maybe lost some momentum," Lightning forward Pat

Center Yanni Gourde (37) and Washington Capitals goaltender Braden Holtby (70) keep a close eye on the puck during the second period of the Lightning's 3-2 shootout win.

Maroon said. "They came back in those five minutes with a push, but I thought we responded well. I thought we were in their face. That's the kind of team we need to be, kind of have that mentality to push back and don't let them run around."

With a different feel to the roster this season, the response was better than perhaps it has been in past playoff performances.

"You have to be able to look another team in the eye and in previous years we haven't done that as well as we should have," Cooper said. "We brought in some players that can help us now in that regard immensely. I like the confidence of our group, we have a don't-back-down attitude which is something that we know we're going to need." ∎

AUGUST 5, 2020 · TORONTO, ONTARIO
LIGHTNING 3, BRUINS 2

PATIENCE PAYS OFF

Lightning Seize Opportunities, Remain Perfect Through Two Games

Through playoffs past, patience and understanding proved fleeting at times for the Tampa Bay Lightning.

Two games into round-robin play in the 2020 Stanley Cup playoffs, the Lightning showed both elements might stick with them this time around.

Tyler Johnson scored on a rebound with under 90 seconds remaining in the third period to lift the Lightning to a 3-2 victory against the Boston Bruins.

With a perfect record through two games, the Lightning showed something different, something that perhaps had victimized them at times in previous postseason appearances. And it served them deep into the playoffs.

Against Boston, Tampa Bay refused to be rattled, refused to force things, refused to give up any space to the Bruins, even when it looked like the game might slip away from them.

The Lightning held a 2-1 lead entering the third period but saw it evaporate less than two minutes in following a Kevin Shattenkirk turnover in the defensive zone. Zdeno Chara turned the mistake into a soft point shot through traffic that handcuffed Andrei Vasilevskiy and trickled through his pads, allowing Chris Wagner to poke the loose puck in at 1:47.

Tampa Bay still refused to be rattled by the events that transpired. They refused to be broken, killing off two power play chances with the game tied in the third. It seems that the Lightning have fully embraced the "Embrace the Suck and Dance in the Rain" philosophy put forth by Lightning general manager Julien BriseBois, which essentially means, "Don't let what you can't control deter you from the goal."

So Tampa Bay just kept working, staying patient, not trying to force the game to go their way.

They didn't feed into the Bruins, typically a team that is structured and patient while waiting for teams to make mistakes. Outside of the Shattenkirk turnover, Tampa Bay played a relatively clean third period. And when the opportunity emerged for the Lightning, they were the team that pounced with 1:27 left in regulation.

As the teams were making line changes, Shattenkirk waited with the puck just above the circles in his own zone and zipped a pass up to Alex Killorn above the Boston blue line. Killorn left a touch pass for a charging Yanni Gourde to gain the zone. Gourde then fired a shot toward Rask's far pad as he kicked the puck out to a barreling Johnson, who had a step on Sean Kuraly, for an open shot he buried for the winner.

"It's just something that happens," Johnson said. "I don't think we necessarily knew it was going to end that way or anything like that. It was just two good plays by

Lightning goaltender Andrei Vasilevskiy makes a save against Boston Bruins center Charlie Coyle during the first period of the 3-2 Lightning win.

those two guys (Killorn and Gourde). They are good hockey players and we were able to make it work."

It all came about because the Lightning let the game come to them and took advantage of the opportunity when it emerged.

"We tried to keep up the positivity on the bench and we have to try to create our energy without any fans here in the building," defenseman Ryan McDonagh said. "Our guys did a good job of slowly getting the momentum back and letting our structure and our decision making with and without the puck take over. It was no coincidence that it was a pretty simple play on the game winner."

McDonagh used three key terms in his comments: structure, decision making and simple. The Lightning want to be able to trust themselves, trust the process and hold a strong belief that less can be more. They didn't overthink, they didn't force plays, they let them develop organically and remained steadfast in that approach. ∎

AUGUST 8, 2020 · TORONTO, ONTARIO
FLYERS 4, LIGHTNING 1

BLUE LINE BLUES

Loss to Flyers Sets Up First-Round Rematch Against Columbus

The result of Tampa Bay's final round-robin game, a 4-1 loss to the Philadelphia Flyers, took a back seat to something that nearly derailed the Lightning's playoff journey before it even got on track.

Midway through the first period, Norris Trophy defenseman Victor Hedman turned to pivot backwards while entering the Lightning zone, and the toe of his skate appeared to get caught in the ice, flexing his right foot and dropping the 6-foot-6 blue liner to his knees. Hedman stayed down on the ice as he continued to slide back toward his own net and kept the right foot slightly elevated off the ice as he slid.

Hedman was able to gingerly skate back to the Lightning bench where he sat briefly. During the ensuing television timeout, Hedman took a twirl on the ice to test the ankle, but it was immediately apparent he would not be able to continue. As he walked back toward the locker room with a noticeable limp, Hedman stopped just before the tunnel and slammed his stick against the glass several times, breaking the stick into pieces.

Before the start of the second period, the team announced that Hedman would not return to the game.

Lightning head coach Jon Cooper did not offer any updates on the nature of the injury or provide insight into the extent of it.

"If you watched the game you can probably figure out what happened," Cooper said. "We don't know how long this is going to be but with Victor, a perennial Norris Trophy finalist every year out, that creates a hole. But we've dealt with injuries before, our captain is out and he's been out for a long time and it's a little frustrating because we feel like we're going in the right direction, then to lose some of the star power that we have, that's why you go out and pick up guys at the deadline to add depth to your team."

Outside of goaltender Andrei Vasilevskiy, Hedman might be the most valuable player on the Lightning's roster. In the game against Philadelphia, his absence was apparent, and the Lightning looked out of sync after he left the game.

"We know the significance of the role that Heddy plays on our team," defenseman Ryan McDonagh said. Hedman "plays in all situations and we love having him out there. It was tough to see, but you have to roll with what happens."

At stake in the game against the Flyers was the top seed in the Eastern Conference, and Tampa Bay came out looking like a team that wanted that top seed. In the opening six minutes of the game, Nikita Kucherov hit the crossbar at 5:04 and on his next shift, picked off an Ivan Provorov pass just inside the Lightning

Tampa Bay Lightning center Anthony Cirelli checks Philadelphia Flyers center Tyler Pitlick into the boards during the 4-1 Flyers win. This was the last tune-up game before Tampa Bay's first-round rematch against Columbus.

blue line for a breakaway, though his attempt to go five-hole was turned aside by Carter Hart.

The Flyers broke the ice with a pair of goals seven minutes apart in the first period before Tyler Johnson pulled one back with a power play goal 5:21 into the second period. Philadelphia regained the two-goal lead with 5:28 left in the second before locking it down in the third and adding an empty-net goal to

secure the top seed for the playoffs, which also set up the Lightning for a first-round rematch with the Columbus Blue Jackets

"I thought the third period there were a lot of good things . . . now we're not pinning medals on our chest for moral victories, but we can build off that as we move forward," Cooper said. "But it's never a bad thing having to eat a piece of humble pie." ∎

AUGUST 11, 2020 · TORONTO, ONTARIO
LIGHTNING 3, BLUE JACKETS 2 (5OT)

MARATHON MEN

Lightning Prove Mettle in Five-Overtime Gauntlet

The eruption of emotion emerging from the Tampa Bay Lightning bench looked as pure and genuine as a puppy frolicking through a freshly cut field chasing a ball.

After 150 minutes and 27 seconds of hockey, Brayden Point whipped a wrist shot from the left circle that zipped in just over the shoulder of Joonas Korpisalo and under the bar of the net, which for most of the game had resembled an impenetrable fortress.

Shot attempt after shot attempt after shot attempt was blocked or stopped until finally on the 187th attempted shot and the 88th that was directed on net, the Tampa Bay Lightning ended the fourth-longest game in NHL history to defeat the Columbus Blue Jackets 3-2 in the fifth overtime, taking a 1-0 series lead in the best-of-seven opening round series.

With each minute added to the game time, record after record started to fall, from ice time to shots on goal to saves. The numbers when all was said and done boggled the mind.

Yet beyond all the numbers and records set is the simple truth of the moment Point scored and elation boiled over along the far boards—the Lightning showed that regardless of the perceptions many have about them, they are a different team than the one that was historically swept aside in 2019.

The way Tuesday's playoff ended will forever be etched in the minds of those who played in it, those who stood behind the bench and the very few that were able to witness it live from Scotiabank Arena in the time of COVID-19.

The memories will live on forever.

"To see the excitement on the players when they scored, regardless if there were fans in the building or not, that's one thing I'll remember as you turn back the clock back and they're still a bunch of kids," Lightning head coach Jon Cooper said. "They compete their (tails) off and they get damn excited when they score and especially when they were in the fifth overtime. It brings you back to the frozen pond. It was a pretty cool moment."

To watch the players, who probably hadn't eaten a meal in 10-12 hours because of the 3 p.m. start time, pour off the bench in elation was magical.

Brayden Point celebrates his game-winning goal against the Columbus Blue Jackets during the fifth overtime of the Game 1 marathon victory.

"It was very special," said Yanni Gourde, whose goal 23 seconds into the third period tied the game 2-2. "I mean at that point we're all exhausted, and we are all hoping for a goal. And when we saw that shot go in it was just emotion and I think it was really fun to be a part of."

What happened in 2019 at the hands of Columbus led to an offseason of soul searching that ran through the entire Lightning hockey operations staff. It led to a shift in playing philosophy and roster building.

They needed to be harder to play against, so they brought in Pat Maroon before the season and added Blake Coleman and Barclay Goodrow in separate deals at the trade deadline.

Then there is the approach to playing the game. There needed to be less risk and more patience. There needed to be better puck management and more focus on the small details of the game, such as coverage in the defensive zone and chipping pucks out of danger instead of forcing plays.

And through what amounted to 2½ games packed in to one, in the opening game of the playoffs no less, that patience and mettle was tested over and over (and over and over and over) again.

Tampa Bay just kept pushing and didn't allow themselves to be diverted from the game plan. In all, the Lightning finished with 187 shot attempts toward the Columbus net, 62 of which were blocked by the Blue Jackets. They kept going to work, shift after shift.

"I think you just tried to stick with the program," said Point, who opened the scoring for Tampa Bay in the first period. "I thought we were getting some good chances but there's no way to prepare for that long. I thought we did a good job of just competing and keeping our feet moving. I think that's just the mindset you need to have, just focus on your next shift and not the end result. Focus on how you're playing and what you have to do."

It's the exact approach the coaching staff has been asking the team to take from the outset of the season all the way up to the pause, and then reemphasized during the two-week camp before arriving in Toronto.

"If there's anything that this team has grown in it's just sticking to the program," Cooper said. "And it's so hard to do when there's so much mental stress. Your body is seizing up and I'm sure there are guys cramping and other things were happening and you have to somehow mentally keep your focus. So what we focused on was just little things and don't sacrifice defense for offense."

It's not the flash-and-dash brand the Lightning played in the past.

"It's staying above the puck, it's getting pucks deep it's doing all the things that aren't flashy," Cooper said. "It's not the most fun way to play but it's the winning way to play, especially if you want to win games like that when the game becomes a little bit of who blinks first and neither team was. So you just have to wait it out." ∎

Blake Coleman (20) drives Columbus Blue Jackets right wing Cam Atkinson (13) into Lightning goaltender Andrei Vasilevskiy (88) during the first period of the grueling Game 1 win.

AUGUST 13, 2020 · TORONTO, ONTARIO
BLUE JACKETS 3, LIGHTNING 1

MISSED CHANCES

Blue Jackets Take Advantage of Lackluster Lightning Play

Momentum is a funny thing. It can make you feel like absolutely everything is working, that the ice is tilted in your favor and the game is going your way.

One moment you're a kid walking out of the candy store with a bag full of Jelly Bellys and a smile as wide as the Gulf of Mexico. You're feeling so good in fact that you fail to notice the step down from the sidewalk, so you fall straight to the ground, skinning your knees, and a hole opens up in the bag of jelly beans causing almost all of them to pour onto the pavement.

You can get back up and start to walk down the sidewalk once again, but the damage is done. There are scrapes and cuts on your legs, you managed to salvage only some of the sugary treat in the bag and that smile has turned upside down.

Tampa Bay Lightning are of course the kid in this metaphor, because coming off a Game 1 thriller the Lightning were riding high. They started Game 2 feeding off that momentum, but it inexplicably disappeared. Before they could recover, the Lightning found themselves trailing and never got even.

Now the series is all even after two games.

"We had an exceptional start and we did everything we wanted to and we dictated play and we scored that first goal," head coach Jon Cooper said. "And to be honest, we might have got a little comfortable and the second that happens to you, you get what happened tonight."

Tampa Bay came out ready to play, had Columbus hemmed in shift after shift and found the lead when Nikita Kucherov found a puck that bounced off the end boards from an Ondrej Palat shot, quickly recovered it and pulled it back to bank a shot in off of Columbus goaltender Joonas Korpisalo 5:24 into the game. By the time the midpoint of the period rolled around, the Lightning had the lead, a 9-0 advantage on the shot clock and were heading to the powerplay with Seth Jones off for tripping at the 10:30 mark.

Everything was turning up Tampa Bay.

And if the Lightning are able to put a second goal in at that point, there's a chance they run away with the game as the amount of hockey the Blue Jackets had played over the previous week looked like it was catching up to them.

But there was no second goal.

That's when the sidewalk snuck up on them.

At this point, the Blue Jackets had yet to even register a shot on goal. But one breakdown, one bad break and a blown coverage on the same play saw Pierre-Luc Dubois tie the game. A power play goal in

Columbus Blue Jackets goaltender Joonas Korpisalo (70) defends the goal as the Tampa Bay Lightning and the Blue Jackets battle in the crease during Game 2. The Lighting only scored once on Korpisalo and the Blue Jackets evened the series at 1-1.

the final minute of the first put the Lightning behind.

All the good will, all that momentum built up evaporated in about 25 seconds.

Alexander Wennberg added a third-period goal, and the Blue Jackets clamped it down from that point to even up the series.

"We just kind of lost our mojo a little bit when we gave up the lead and in particular spurts we got it back but just not with the same consistency we had the other night," Cooper said. "And you know when you give really good team like Columbus a chance to get back into it and they took advantage of it. We just couldn't find a way to come back and it wasn't to say we didn't have our chances because we had some glorious ones. But some nights they're not going to go in and tonight was that night." ∎

AUGUST 15, 2020 · TORONTO, ONTARIO
LIGHTNING 3, BLUE JACKETS 2

STICK TO THE PLAN

Lightning Stay In Control as Series Tilts Their Way

Clinical precision.

That's how the Tampa Bay Lightning closed out the final two periods of a 3-2 victory in Game 3 against the Columbus Blue Jackets to take a 2-1 lead in the series.

In a series the Lightning have all but dominated on several levels, they maintained form, limiting mistakes and suffocating any attack the Blue Jackets attempted to make, and in the process finding a way to get some pucks past Joonas Korpisalo, who was starting to conjure up whispers of the phrase "Halaked" (Google it) with the way he was snuffing out Tampa Bay's offense.

The underlying numbers, plus a little good fortune while having to kill off three early power plays, show just how dominant the Lightning were in Game 3. It's a trend that, if it continues, bodes well for the rest of the series.

Through the first two games, the Lightning won many of the predictive statistical battles which provide insight as to how a game, or series, will play out. All the numbers—shot attempts, scoring chances, high danger chances, etc.—favored Tampa Bay with ratings above 60-percent in all categories.

Despite the setbacks in their previous game, the Lightning remained on task, not looking to make any drastic changes in response to a loss.

They did make one lineup change, inserting Carter Verhaeghe in place of Mitchell Stephens on the fourth line. Everything else remained the same, in the belief that keeping with the way things were going would pay off.

"I think we've had plenty of chances, we haven't executed the way that we have in the past, but at some point it's going to go in for you," Lightning head coach Jon Cooper said. "It just doesn't happen every single game for you."

It took some hard work at the start of the game to get the ball rolling as the Blue Jackets had three power plays in the opening 10 minutes of the game, including 1:26 of a 5-on-3 power play the Lightning were able to survive and escape with a 0-0 score.

"That's the thing with five-on-threes, especially in the playoffs they can create momentum either

Blue Jackets right wing Oliver Bjorkstrand (28) falls to the ice after being tripped by Tampa Bay Lightning defenseman Zach Bogosian (24) during the first period of the Lightning's Game 3 win.

way," forward Alex Killorn said. "I think for us, we're fortunate the one hits the post, but when you kill those off it creates such a momentum for your team going forward. I was so impressed with the guys that killed those penalties but even happier with the way we played after that."

From then on, apart from a couple of turnovers, the Lightning were clinical in how they went about their game. They were rewarded in the first period after a rare Columbus neutral zone mistake when Liam Foudy's attempted pass went off the shin pad of Zach Bogosian to spring Killorn off on a 2-on-1 rush the other way with Anthony Cirelli. As David Savard dropped to his stomach to take away the passing lane, Killorn faked the pass and slipped a backhand pass under the pads of Korpisalo at 15:48 for a 1-0 lead.

"It's kind of just a two-on-one quick play and their D made a good move sliding," Killorn said. "Then I kind of saw their goalie kind of sliding over and just found the five hole and was able to put in in off the backhand."

Though Columbus tied it early in the second on a breakdown that led to a Riley Nash goal, the Lightning controlled the rest of the game. Brayden Point put Tampa Bay in front getting inside the Columbus defense to convert a rebound from Ryan McDonagh's shot at 14:16.

Victor Hedman made it 3-1 late in the period, cutting down the middle to take a pass from Verhaeghe and zip a shot through Korpisalo with 1:07 left in the second period.

It was a just reward for the work the Lightning had put in, not just in the game, but the series.

"I thought we were very good with the puck today," Hedman said. "I think the second or third period was the way we want to play. We made it harder on them and we limited them to three shots in the third and we had them chasing. So obviously very happy with the way we responded."

The Lightning are a team that is prone to mismanaging the puck at times, harkening back to last year's Game 1 against Columbus when they blew a three-goal lead and lost in regulation. After that game, Cooper said his team was too worried about scoring the fourth goal instead of preventing the first one against.

On Saturday, the giveaways were limited to just five.

"We've had some pretty good runs with possessing the puck but we were responsible and that's a big part," Cooper said. "You can always possess it but if you're reckless with it, it can turn into problems and we were pretty responsible with the puck. I'm not saying we were perfect—obviously gave up a couple odd-man rushes—but for the most part the we had really good mojo going on the bench. Every line was getting involved even in the third when they get the second one early, I thought you know instead of kind of gripping our sticks we played loose."

And if that's how Tampa Bay is going to continue to play, it bodes well for the rest of the series. ■

Lightning head coach Jon Cooper (left) reacts after getting the key Game 3 victory.

AUGUST 17, 2020 · TORONTO, ONTARIO
LIGHTNING 2, BLUE JACKETS 1

HARD TO HANDLE

Tampa Bay 'Gnats' Demonstrate Power of Persistence

Anybody who spends more than a few minutes outdoors in Florida knows the feeling of having to incessantly wave your hand around to create enough moving air to dissuade those annoying aerial midge bugs from buzzing around.

But each motion (which seems like it should bring Hurricane force air currents to insects the size of a pin head) only offers temporary relief. They return to the scene time and time again. No matter how many times you wave your hand, no matter the force you summon to create a breeze, they just won't go away.

May we present for your viewing pleasure the Tampa Bay Lightning equivalent: the Gnat Line, featuring the trio of Yanni Gourde, Blake Coleman and Barclay Goodrow.

The trio, which logged a total of one minute and 21 seconds together in the regular season, is a big reason why Tampa Bay has a 3-1 series lead against the Columbus Blue Jackets and is on the cusp of advancing to the second round of the postseason for the fourth time in the past six years.

Tampa Bay's third line accounted for both goals in a 2-1 victory against Columbus in Game 4, with Goodrow scoring his first goal in a Lightning sweater while Gourde notched his second of the series. Along with Coleman, the line combined for five points, plus-6, and had 10 of the Lightning's 22 shots on goal in the game.

They were rewarded in Game 4 for their strong play in the series to this point.

Head coach Jon Cooper has tabbed the trio to be the starting line in 17 of the 18 periods of play through four games. The only period the line has not taken the opening draw was the second period of Game 1, making 16 consecutive periods the Gnats have started things off with a buzz. And twice they have scored on the opening shift of a period—23 seconds into the third period in Game 1 to tie the game and 16 seconds into the second period of Game 4 to open the scoring.

"They do set the tone for us," Cooper said. "I feel like they're always just buzzing around and you're trying to knock them away but just never leave. They're pests."

Blue Jackets right wing Cam Atkinson gets bumped by Tampa Bay Lightning defenseman Mikhail Sergachev as he celebrates his goal during the second period of the Game 4 Tampa Bay win.

In Game 4, the trio logged the most ice time at even strength with 12 minutes and 19 seconds, and they were far and away Tampa Bay's most effective line beyond just the goals. They had a 14-5 advantage in shot attempts (73 percent CORSI), which came while matched up most of the game against Columbus's top defensive pairing of Seth Jones and Zach Werenski. The 14 shot attempts equaled the combined number of the Lightning's first two lines.

The success stems from their simple and similar approach.

"We just try to keep our game pretty simple," Gourde said. "We know what works for us, we chip it in, we're all three around the puck, simple plays and it works for us."

"I think we're all similar players," Goodrow said. "We're not the fanciest players, we all like to work off the forechek and get pucks in and deep and be responsible out there. We've been able to read off each other so far and found a little bit of chemistry here."

Through the four games in the series they have been as dominant as one line could possibly be. In 91:25 of even strength time together, they own 67-percent of the shot attempts, holding a 108-53 advantage, and 73-percent of the expected goal rate.

Wait, it gets better. The Gnats have 70-percent of the scoring chances while on the ice, 49-21, and an astounding 77-percent of the high danger chances, with a 20-6 advantage.

"I think there's a lot of predictability in our game and that makes it easy and it makes it fun to play with these guys," Coleman said. "I know what I'm going to get from them night in and night out. They're always in on the forecheck. I don't think I've been the F3 (third forward in the zone) this much in my life but it makes it easy to play with these guys and it's been fun."

When reboot camp started on July 13, the three were placed together and haven't looked back.

"A lot of it is your feel and we've put other lines together that work, too," Cooper said. "I just like the mentality of the three. They just they compete so hard and they never really get themselves in trouble."

It's a big part of why Cooper writes their line down on the lineup sheet for the start of every period. And more often than not, the puck gets in deep and they go to work.

"Their effort and their play . . . it bleeds into our team," defenseman Kevin Shattenkirk said. "I think the key is that they haven't strayed from the game play, they realize what makes them good and they realize what makes their line successful and what works. The fact that they've started to see some success and they haven't started to cheat for any offense, they stick with the game plan."

It's that relentless approach and never giving up, you know, like those tiny insects that just don't go away.

"I think they realized that they're just a really annoying line," Shattenkirk said. "And they're a tough line to play against other teams, they are always in guys' faces . . . they don't really give you a lot of room. So for us they're definitely a line that energizes us when things might not be going our way, we know we can count on them." ∎

Blue Jackets left wing Nick Foligno (left) gets dumped into the net by Tampa Bay Lightning defenseman Zach Bogosian (24) as goaltender Andrei Vasilevskiy (88) deals with Jackets center Boone Jenner (38). Vasilevskiy only allowed one goal as the Lightning took control of the series in Game 4.

AUGUST 19, 2020 · TORONTO, ONTARIO
LIGHTNING 5, BLUE JACKETS 4 (OT)

EXCLAMATION POINT

Lightning Find Redemption with First-Round Success

Demons Out!

Sixteen months after being historically swept out of the playoffs in the opening round, the Tampa Bay Lightning found a form of retribution against the Columbus Blue Jackets.

Tampa Bay shook off a dreadful second period performance and rallied from two goals down in the third period to force overtime, where Brayden Point proved the hero for the second time in the series. The 5-4 victory sent the Lightning into the second round of the NHL Playoffs for the fourth time in six years.

Tampa Bay moved past Columbus in five difficult games, two determined in overtime, to find redemption a season later.

As Lightning head coach Jon Cooper finished with the handshake line and turned back toward the home bench, he pumped a celebratory fist in the air, pushing out more than a year of pent up emotion.

"We had 422 days to think about it, but who's counting," Cooper said.

Cooper pumping his fist in the air as he walked off the ice. It clearly signified more than just the routine playoff series victory, even more still than the 2015 second round victory against the Montreal Canadiens one year after being swept by Montreal in the first round the year before.

"It's funny how the hockey gods work," Cooper said. "You go through what we did last year and then get second-guessed on a lot of things we did. We go through the season. Then we have the pause and everything that's happened. Then, during reseeding and the new rules and all those things, still end up playing the same team . . . it's easy to sit up here and say you wanted them, but it was good to get them and good to get this result."

And for the many who have wondered whether the humble pie the Lightning were fed last season led to any lessons learned, the proof was in the result.

"A lot of learning went into last year," Cooper said. "We had to grow as a team, we didn't necessarily need to tweak how we play the game as much on structure

Brayden Point celebrates after scoring the series-winning goal during overtime of Game 5, his second overtime goal of the series.

as it was between the ears. And all of us collectively, from the coaching staff all the way down, had to be better and we had to train ourselves to play a little bit of a different way and we did. In the end you can lay a plan out to your players, but players have to play, they're the ones that decide it and they deserve the credit for it."

The path in the clinching game was not exactly smooth, it was more of a country road riddled with rocks, potholes and detours. But it still led to the same destination.

After grabbing a two-goal lead in the first period on goals 61 seconds apart by Tyler Johnson and Blake Coleman, the game looked like it was going to be easy. Even after Columbus pulled one back one second after a power play expired, Tampa Bay did not look in trouble.

But the second period was, to be blunt, atrocious, as Columbus had an astounding 42 total shot attempts while the Lightning had 10.

Tampa Bay was fortunate to come out of the period only down 3-2, and it took a goal in the final minute of the period to give Columbus the lead after assaulting the Lightning net with 24 shots.

"We didn't manage it well in the second," defenseman Kevin Shattenkirk said. "I think we were playing on our heels a bit and you have to also realize that they're playing for their lives out there, playing for their season. We got out of (the period) luckily with only a one goal deficit."

Shattenkirk, who delivered a message to settle the team down during the second intermission, stepped up on the ice as well. After the Jackets went up by two, Shattenkirk pulled the Lightning back to within a goal with 7:59 left in the third.

"You close the lead to just one goal with still a fair amount of time left it certainly gives the team a little bit of life," Shattenkirk said. "And it could have come from anyone on the ice or anyone on the bench to get it but all we were thinking there was 'just get one and keep going.'"

The tying goal did come as the Lightning pressed, with Brayden Point putting a puck toward the crease that banked in off the skate of Anthony Cirelli with 1:38 left on the clock and forced the second overtime game of the series

Also for the second time in the series, it was Point who proved to be the hero.

In an overtime dominated by the Lightning, Nikita Kucherov took advantage of a puck that caromed off the skate of Columbus defenseman Vladislav Gavrikov by quickly scooping it up and finding Point alone in front of the net. Point made a quick hesitation to get Korpisalo down before lifting a backhand into the net to decide the game and the series at 5:12.

Point became the second player in franchise history to score an overtime, series-clinching goal, joining Martin St. Louis, who did it twice.

Point, who ended the epic five-overtime affair in Game 1, became just the 18th player in NHL history to score two overtime goals in the same series. The last to do it was Mikkel Boedker with the Phoenix Coyotes in the 2012 Conference Quarterfinals against the Blackhawks. ◾

Kevin Shattenkirk checks Blue Jackets left wing Nick Foligno into the boards during Game 5, as Tampa Bay exacts revenge on Columbus from their 2019 playoff matchup and knocks them out of the playoffs.

AUGUST 23, 2020 · TORONTO, ONTARIO
BRUINS 3, LIGHTNING 2

AN EARLY HOLE

Tentative Start Dooms Lightning as Bruins Take Series Opener

There are not many early holes the Tampa Bay Lightning crawl out of with a deep offensive attack. But in the playoffs, one can't afford to test things out for too long or a series can get short early.

And now, after a 3-2 loss to the Boston Bruins, the Lightning are down 1-0 in the best-of-seven, second-round series.

What perhaps was most surprising about the start on Tampa Bay's part was how tentative the Lightning looked.

Six games into the playoffs, even in these most unusual circumstances, is not exactly early in the postseason. There should be some intensity right off the bat, or at least a more focused approach to the game.

On top of that, the Lightning are facing division rival Boston and there is enough familiarity between the two sides that there should be no surprises.

But for whatever reason, Tampa Bay looked tentative. The Lightning were so hesitant at times, it conjured up thoughts of the second period of Game 5 against Columbus in the opening round.

"It was extremely disappointing to be honest," Lightning head coach Jon Cooper said. "We just had that type of a period against Columbus in our last game and that was dreadful. I thought our first period

tonight was along those lines."

All the patience that Tampa Bay showed in the opening-round series victory against Columbus turned to impatience. All the positive puck management the Lightning displayed throughout most of the first round against the Blue Jackets, well, it wasn't very positive.

"I thought it was pretty sloppy the way we started," forward Tyler Johnson said. "We got better as the game went on, but I still think overall we were a lot sloppier than we are normally."

For an experienced team that should know exactly what to expect, it was inexcusable.

"We're obviously disappointed with the way we came out in the first," defenseman Victor Hedman said. "We expect more of ourselves and we know that wasn't good enough in the first. So that one period and I wouldn't say it lost us a game but they were able to take advantage of that. So that's on us in that room to be better."

Boston built the lead on a first period goal from Charlie Coyle, a power play goal from David Pastrnak in the second and an early third-period goal from Brad Marchand.

The Lightning did have enough positive elements to their game, particularly in the second period when

Bruins center David Krejci rides Lightning goaltender Andrei Vasilevskiy as the Lightning try to clear the puck during the third period.

they spent nearly the final 15 minutes in the Boston end. They peppered the Bruins' crease area and wound up with a 34-16 shot attempt advantage and a pair of Victor Hedman goals did bring the Lightning to within a goal.

But in the playoffs, a loss is a loss.

"There are no moral victories, only lessons learned," Cooper said. "And we learned that if you are going to beat the President's Trophy team you have to play a full sixty minutes." ■

AUGUST 25, 2020 · TORONTO, ONTARIO
LIGHTNING 4, BRUINS 3 (OT)

DANCING IN THE RAIN

Palat's Overtime Winner Knots Series at One

In July, when the NHL was on the verge of returning to action, Lightning general manager Julien BriseBois discussed roster selection and the team's approach to the Return to Play Stanley Cup Tournament.

"We're going to embrace the suck and dance in the rain," BriseBois said at the time.

Well, in Game 2 of the Eastern Conference semifinals against the Boston Bruins, it started to rain. And by the end, it was the Lightning that were doing the dancing after Ondrej Palat's overtime winner knotted the best-of-seven series at one game each.

What BriseBois meant when he uttered the phrase boils down to not worrying about things that are out of one's control. Whatever happens, don't let it affect the approach the team wants to embrace in these playoffs. Keep pushing forward and control what you can control.

"If you want to have any chance of winning and going deep in the playoffs, adversity strikes in the weirdest ways," Lightning head coach Jon Cooper said. "You never know when it's going to happen

and sometimes you just eat a...sandwich...you know what I mean."

Tampa Bay was served one of those *cough, cough* sandwiches even before the game as top defeseman Ryan McDonagh was unable to play and the Lightning were forced to make lineup changes, really for the first time in the playoffs, dressing seven defensemen as Braydon Coburn and Luke Schenn made their playoff debut.

It didn't phase the Lightning one bit as Tampa Bay did exactly what they wanted to do at the start of the game and were all over the Bruins.

Then, Tampa Bay had to take a couple of bites out of that metaphorical sandwich Cooper referred to because fortune reversed in a hurry when Zach Bogosian took a shot at the right point at the 3:03 mark only to have his stick snap in half, leaving him helpless to defend as the Bruins were able to quickly counter and create a 2-on-1. After an initial miss, Nick Ritchie stuffed the puck through the pads of Andrei Vasilevskiy and put Boston up 1-0.

The Lightning considered challenging the play for

Lightning left wing Ondrej Palat (18) celebrates with teammate Patrick Maroon (14) after scoring the game-winning goal in overtime of the Game 2 win over the Bruins.

92

goalie interference but opted not to take the chance and risk a power play chance against. Less than two minutes later, the Lightning thought they tied the game on a deflection from Barclay Goodrow. But Boston challenged the play for offside and review showed that Brayden Point had not quite cleared the zone on a tag-up play as Goodrow entered to get in on the forecheck.

Embracing the suck, however, means to move past what's not going your way.

"I think we were playing well enough that it really didn't faze us, it was a matter of time before we're going to get another one," forward Blake Coleman said. "I think we were kind of carrying the play in the first and when you're playing well it's easy to stay up and positive. The response was good and every time we hit adversity at any point in this game I thought we had an answer."

Coleman had that first answer.

As Bogosian rushed up ice to start the play, he split Torey Krug and Brandon Carlo just inside the Boston blue line. As Bogosian was falling forward to the ice, he was able to slide a pass over to a charging Coleman who launched forward while doing a superman impersonation to swat the puck past Jaroslav Halak.

The Lightning fell behind on a Brad Marchand power play goal at 14:33 of the second period, but that was answered 55 seconds later on a Nikita Kucherov goal, getting his stick on a Kevin Shattenkirk shot. The play started with Brayden Point dancing away from a couple of defenders and spinning off the wall, pulling the puck back from Anders Bjork to set up Shattenkirk.

Coleman was at it again in the third, getting behind the Boston defense to take a brilliant stretch pass from Victor Hedman to get in on a breakaway with his partially disrupted shot pinballing off the pads of Halak for a 3-2 lead with 9:20 in the third.

The Bruins didn't fold and answered back when Tyler Johnson was unable to corral a puck high in the zone for a possible clear. Seconds later Marchand was open at the post for a backdoor play on a pass from Sean Kuraly to tie things up with 3:58 left to play.

It was pouring rain, again, and Tampa Bay was force to take another bite out of that very soggy sandwich.

Embrace and dance.

"If there was one message that was going on it was that we liked everything that was going on about the game," Cooper said. "I know it sounds so cliche, but we had stick with it. If you have mental weakness at all you're probably sitting there saying you're sorry for us but that's not how we operate. Anytime something goes against us, just turn the page. It was needed tonight."

In overtime, the Lightning danced. And danced. And danced.

With an aggressive approach, Tampa Bay put constant pressure on the Bruins and 4:40 into the overtime, Palat found a puck loose near the right post after Pat Maroon made a power move from behind the net to the front to set it up.

"I was just very happy," Palat said. "I'm seeing Patty and I just screamed and I was just very happy. I don't know what I did. I was just very happy for a team." ■

Bruins left wing Brad Marchand (63) checks Tampa Bay Lightning center Anthony Cirelli (71) during the first period of Game 2.

AUGUST 26, 2020 · TORONTO, ONTARIO
LIGHTNING 7, BRUINS 1

'JUST ONE WIN'

Dominant Performance Shifts Momentum to Lightning

Hockey is not soccer. There is no aggregate score to determine the winner of a series. If it were, the Tampa Bay Lightning would have a near insurmountable lead on the Boston Bruins through three games after a lopsided 7-1 result in Game 3 of the second round, best-of-seven series.

In the end, however, it only counts as one victory to provide a 2-1 series lead. But what a victory it turned out.

Playing on consecutive nights, Tampa Bay found a spark from a previous lifeless power play that sat in an 0-for-16 stretch, including to start off Game 3.

Ah, but that second chance. And the third chance. Oh, and the fourth chance.

Yeah, it caught fire and it finally burned the Bruins.

"Well at some point they have to break out right," Lightning head coach Jon Cooper said. "The Boston Bruins have a vote, too, they're trying to stop us so they've got a plan and they execute a plan. Then we have to adjust our plan and tonight it worked out."

That adjustment came from moving Kucherov to the opposite circle from where he normally operates, swapping with Ondrej Palat. It provided a much different look not just from the different locations on the ice for the two players, but for how the power play operated with Kucherov quarterbacking the show off the half boards.

So instead of Mikhail Sergachev running things from the point, shifting the puck from side-to-side and occasionally trying to bomb shots from the blue line, Kucherov ran the show.

On the first goal the Bruins stayed tight to Kucherov at the circle, but he was able to quickly get a pass back to Sergachev, who fed Palat for a one-timer that nipped the stick of Zdeno Chara and found the top corner for a 1-0 lead at 12:46 of the first period.

Yanni Gourde, with the help of a pick play set unintentionally by the linesman, made it 2-0 just 15 seconds later, marking the fastest two goals scored in franchise playoff history.

But the second power play goal of the game

Ondrej Palat celebrates his first-period goal with teammate Mikhail Sergachev. Palat's goal was the first strike of the Lightning's seven-goal onslaught.

provided the different look as Kucherov carried the puck down low to the bottom of the circle. As he floated down with the puck, it forced the Boston penalty killers down low with him with created open space up top for him to quickly turn and put a puck right in the path of Sergachev who had an open seam to laser a shot past Halak for a 3-0 lead.

After the Bruins pulled a goal back, Kucherov gave another different look to set up the third power play goal, circling from outside the blue line to generate speed. As he reentered, Kucherov took a pass from Sergachev and attacked the circle, drawing Joakim Nordstrom to him. As he was able to make a quick move to his left to elude Nordstrom's, a seam opened up and Kucherov found Palat across the seam. As Palat took a stride in and put a shot on net, Alex Killorn popped the rebound in on his backhand to regain the three-goal lead for Tampa Bay at 8:35 of the second period.

"Last game we definitely had a lot more opportunities especially our second or third power play and we had confidence going off that," Killorn said of the power play. "It seems like it's been a little while since we scored and I know guys we're getting a little frustrated at times. But tonight was a great night for confidence. When you get a couple it helps you momentum-wise."

For all intents and purposes, the game was over at that point. On back-to-back nights the Bruins were not going to find the energy needed to erase the deficit.

Boston head coach Bruce Cassidy all but announced that when he removed Halak and replaced him with rookie Dan Vladar, who made his NHL debut, with 8:42 left in the second period. The Bruins did their rookie netminder no favors as

Brayden Point came in on a breakaway at 15:23 for a 5-1 lead and minutes later Gourde raced in alone before putting a shot wide, but Killorn was there for the rebound that caromed off the end boards for a 6-1 lead with 1:59 left in the period.

Kucherov added another early in the third as Tampa Bay finished the night with seven goals, the most Boston has allowed in a playoff game since Buffalo beat the Bruins 9-3 in the opening round of the 1992 playoffs.

By the end of the night the game was already pushed aside. The seven goals look good on the scoresheet, it pads some of the stats and certainly makes the fan base puff out their chests a little bit with pride.

But just as there are no moral victories in losses, there are no quality points for wins. The win only counts as one that put the Lightning up 2-1 in the series.

Remember that roller coaster situation that keeps coming up? Well, it's not just after losses, where it feels like the weight of competition is going to crumble around and bring the season to an end. It's also after victories, of any kind, but particularly where everything is seemingly going well.

"Let's be honest, this is an aberration, it doesn't happen in playoff hockey," Cooper said. "You turn the page on this one, just like you turn the page on an overtime thriller. You can't hang your hat on that one. They're both just one win and we're only halfway there. It's a funny game and you can't just ride the emotions too high or too low, it's just one win." ■

Boston's Brad Marchand battles Tampa Bay defenseman Luke Schenn in front of the Lightning goal during the second period of Game 3.

AUGUST 29, 2020 · TORONTO, ONTARIO
LIGHTNING 3, BRUINS 1

WEATHERING THE STORM

Patience for Palat Pays Off as Lightning Take Game 4

There certainly proved to be a lot to digest coming out of Saturday's Game 4 between the Tampa Bay Lightning and the Boston Bruins.

From the second-longest goal scoring streak in franchise playoff history, Victor Hedman's "big bomb from the blueline" that, in reality, was the opposite, a great goaltending performance getting overshadowed and signs of a maturing team.

All of it added up to 3-1 Lightning victory and a 3-1 commanding series lead against the Boston Bruins.

It all starts with Ondrej Palat. Early in the playoffs he had a slow start offensively. Through the three pre-playoff games and the series against Columbus, Palat had just two assists. This despite the success of linemates Nikita Kucherov and Brayden Point.

Some wondered whether a change of linemates needed to take place. But Jon Cooper tends to be patient with players that have been performers in the past. Well, that patience has paid off in the series against the Bruins.

Palat has points in all four games in the series and, after his two-goal performance in Game 4, a pair of game-winning goals. Palat scored the overtime winner in Game 2 that tied the series, opened the scoring with a power play goal in Game 3 and scored the first two goals of the game on Saturday.

With goals in three consecutive games, Palat is one game shy of matching the franchise playoff record. The multi-goal game was the third of his playoff career and first since Game 3 of the 2018 second round against Boston. He also recorded his 25th career playoff goal to move past Lecavalier and tie Alex Killorn for fourth most in franchise playoff history.

"Pally is a confident player," said Point, who extended his scoring streak to five games and has points in 11 of 12 games. "He's got tons of skill. He's super reliable for us, always in the right spot, he's got tons of skill, he sees the ice well and he's got a heck of a shot. To see a couple go in for him now is awesome and hopefully he can keep that rolling."

Hedman provided some insurance late in the

Ondrej Palat celebrates his second goal of the game. Palat scored the first two goals of the Lightning's 3-1 win.

second period with a key power play goal.

Tampa Bay was on a five-minute power play after a boarding major on Boston's Nick Ritchie for a hit from behind on Yanni Gourde.

Boston had done strong work for most of the five minutes until Victor Hedman finally broke through with less than a minute remaining on the man advantage that put Tampa Bay up 3-0 at the time.

"Big blast from the blue line, and super excited that went in," Hedman said. "That was big for us. You've got to capitalize when you have that opportunity on a five-minute power play. That was huge."

Except, it wasn't really a big blast. While it was a blast off his stick, it actually hit the skate of Par Lindholm, popped up in the air and wound up behind Jaroslav Halak and into the net. While it may not have been a big blast, it was a big goal to ensure momentum did not swing in Boston's favor.

"I thought the Bruins were doing a heck of a job killing the penalty, for the first three minutes or so," Cooper said. "The message on the bench was let's build some momentum off this power play regardless if we score. Then we eventually get a good bounce, a fortunate bounce, and score. The wind goes out of their sails a little bit when that happens because now two (goal lead) is three. But the one thing is... you don't want to lose your momentum on that five because another team can build momentum off that."

Andrei Vasilevsky, meanwhile, came up with another strong effort in net for Tampa Bay, stopping 29 of 30 shots, dropping his goals against average to 1.98 and increasing his save percentage to .927. With Palat's two goals in the game and Tampa Bay grabbing a 3-1 lead in the series, Vasilevskiy's performance was somewhat overlooked, but for the second consecutive game, Vasilevskiy did not let in a goal at even strength.

"It obviously helps having the best goalie in the league back there making some big saves for us," Hedman said.

The Lightning, who have been guilty in playoff years past of concentrating a little too much at the offensive net, have been helping out their netminder.

Tampa Bay has shown throughout the early stages of the playoffs that the lessons of playoffs past are starting to be realized. In the third period, while holding a three-goal lead, they showed that once again they know how to keep things under control. Other than three power play chances that had to be killed off – Boston did convert on the last opportunity with one second left on the power play – the rest of the period the Lightning did not get put under much pressure, limiting Boston to just two shots at 5-on-5 play.

"We weathered the storm when they were pressing, especially on their power play," Lightning head coach Jon Cooper said. "Guys were committed, guys blocking shots, guys were committed to our structure in the neutral zone.... It was a pretty gutty effort here by the guys to shut them down those last five, six minutes." ∎

Bruins left wing Joakim Nordstrom is squeezed into the net during the second period. Lightning goaltender Andrei Vasilevskiy stopped 29 of 30 shots.

AUGUST 31, 2020 • TORONTO, ONTARIO
LIGHTNING 3, BRUINS 2 (2OT)

REFUSE TO LOSE

After 95 Minutes, Hedman's Goal Seals Series Win

The Tampa Bay Lightning and defenseman Victor Hedman refused to be denied a trip to the Eastern Conference finals.

In the second overtime, 95 minutes into Game 5 against the Boston Bruins, Hedman clinched Tampa Bay's fourth trip to the East finals in the past six years.

Coming off the bench on a defensive change, Hedman jumped right into the play, cutting down low from the right side of the ice to pick up a rebound and circle behind the net. Making his way back to the point after giving up the puck to Kevin Shattenkirk, Hedman received the puck back, took a shot that was blocked, and raced down to recover his own rebound for another attempt that was blocked.

But as he did at various points in the second round series against Boston, Hedman used his will and determination to make things happen for the Lightning. After taking another pass from Shattenkirk, Hedman took two strides down from the left circle, took a quick curl drag of the puck before snapping off a shot through the legs of Bruins defenseman Brandon Carlo and under the arms of goaltender Jaroslav Halak.

Hedman's fourth goal of the series came at the 14:10 mark of the second overtime period to give Tampa Bay a 3-2 victory.

That display epitomized the Tampa Bay Lightning through two rounds of these playoffs.

Through two rounds of the 2020 playoffs, Tampa Bay Lightning posted a record of 8-2 first knocking off the Columbus Blue Jackets and now the Bruins. But those opening two rounds of the playoffs have been won, not through superior talent or skill – though there is plenty of that to go around on this roster.

The success to the point has come through commitment, patience and will.

Of the eight wins, six of them have been one-goal wins – which includes the first five wins – and four of them have come in overtime. Two of those have come in multiple overtimes.

For a team that had their mental toughness questioned from past failures, particularly the final two games of the 2018 conference finals and the four-

Lightning defenseman Victor Hedman celebrates with teammates (from left) Ondrej Palat, Patrick Maroon and Alex Killorn after Hedman scored the game-winning goal in the second overtime.

game disaster to open the playoffs last year, they have certainly shown a different mindset.

"A little bit of different personnel on the ice, but the way we play, we haven't really changed too much, it's just maybe our mentality has changed a little bit," Hedman said. "We pay more attention all over the ice, we take pride in the way we play defense, how we play as a group all over the ice. We don't need to score four or five goals every night and then hope (goaltender Andrei Vasilevskiy) bails us out. It's just a constant effort and determination to play better defensively has been a huge turnaround for us. I think everyone in that room feels comfortable with the way we play and everybody knows their role, everyone knows what is expected of them. We're a well balanced team and we're very much looking forward to playing in the next round."

The Lightning are playing in the next round because of everything Hedman mentioned.

It's familiar territory for the Lightning but discovered through a different path to get there.

And how the Lightning dispatched the Bruins shows exactly that. Tampa Bay's play at even strength is a true strength. The aggregate scoring of the series favored the Lightning 19-10 (and the 7-1 win in Game 3 is a big reason for some of that disparity). But at even strength play, Tampa Bay outscored Boston 14-5.

In five games in the series, the Lightning allowed just five even strength goals. And that is a winning formula.

Getting the chance to face off against the Columbus Blue Jackets, after what happened last year, was a sort of validation for the team's new approach and mentality.

"I think it was a good thing that we got to face Columbus first for the guys who were here last year," defenseman Ryan McDonagh said. "We really needed to dial in our focus there, we needed everybody and that's the only way we win games is to get contributions from everybody and everybody buying in. It's a credit to our coaching staff to be able to put guys in positions to be successful. It's just a great attitude, whether it's the new guys coming in or the experience of last year, probably a combination of both. And the great job the coaching staff has done keeping our focus, especially in this bubble here and we've really become a family."

Tampa Bay was able to do it without captain Steven Stamkos, who has yet to return following core muscle surgery he underwent in March and has not been heard from since July 27. For three games in this series, McDonagh was missing due to injury before returning on Monday.

And for most of the game on Monday, Nikita Kucherov was absent after taking a high stick to the chin/jaw area from Boston's Zdeno Chara in the first period. Kucherov returned for the second, but only played four minutes before leaving for the rest of the game.

In the end, though, the absence of Kucherov proved to be just another obstacle to push past with their new-found approach and mentality.

"If you want to advance, you have to win these games. That's all there is to it," Cooper said. "It was gutsy. I'm proud of this team. They've done everything we've asked of them this year." ∎

Lightning goaltender Andrei Vasilevskiy makes a save during the first period of Game 5. Vasilevskiy stopped 45 of 47 shots in the series-clinching win.

SEPTEMBER 7, 2020 · EDMONTON, ALBERTA
LIGHTNING 8, ISLANDERS 2

MESMERIZING

Tampa Bay Defies the Laws of Physics in Dominant Game 1 Win

What we witnessed in Game 1 of the Eastern Conference finals was mesmerizing.

What we saw was beyond the scope of rational thought.

And no matter how many times it's watched it still defies the laws of hockey physics.

There were a ton of possible storylines floating around by the time the Tampa Bay Lightning put the finishing touches on an 8-2 victory against the New York Islanders to grab a 1-0 series lead.

One might zero in on the incredible performances by Brayden Point (two goals, three assists) and Nikita Kucherov (goal, four assists). Or the three power play goals scored by Tampa Bay, two coming with Victor Hedman manning the point.

So much went on in the game, even Yanni Gourde's first goal was an afterthought. The shot went in and out of the net so fast after the puck hit the stick of Andy Greene that play continued until the goal horn went off about a minute later to stop

play after video review confirmed the puck did cross the goal line.

All of those are worthy angles to pursue in a game in which the Lightning matched a playoff franchise record for goals in a game – the most allowed by the Islanders in a playoff game since May 15, 1980 – or how Tampa Bay became the first team to score eight goals in a conference final game since Chicago against Edmonton in 1992.

Then there are all the individual records broken during the game, including Ondrej Palat who scored for the fifth consecutive game to set a new franchise playoff record. Or Kucherov and Point becoming the first pair of teammates to register five points in a conference final game since Jari Kurri and Paul Coffey for Edmonton in 1985. Or Kucherov reaching 16 assists to set a franchise mark for most in a playoff season.

No, it was the play made on the sixth goal of the game by Tampa Bay that resulted in wide-eyed awe.

The sheer brilliance of the entire sequence, highlighted by a remarkable touch pass put on

Ondrej Palat celebrates after getting the puck past Islanders goaltender Thomas Greiss in the first period. Palat scored for the fifth consecutive game to set a new Lightning playoff record.

display by Kucherov at center ice, was a marvel to enjoy and in many ways, defies a proper description of how it played out.

Like most great plays, it started in the Lightning defensive zone.

From the left point, New York defenseman Devon Toews attempted a diagonal pass down low intended for Brock Nelson. But Kucherov was able to deflect the pass with his stick and direct the puck to Kevin Shattenkirk.

Both Kucherov and Point turned up ice to start the rush as Shattenkirk delivered a saucer pass toward Kucherov. Now, here's where a hockey genius takes over because Kucherov did something so subtle that it was barely detectable at full speed.

With the puck racing in his direction, Kucherov turns over the blade of his stick so that it's flat against the ice with the toe facing back in the opposite direction he is skating. The puck then hits the heel of Kucherov's blade and acts as a mini ramp of sorts directing it right to Point along the right-wing boards.

As Point collects the puck, Kucherov continues to drive toward the net with a stride on Nick Leddy and is in the perfect spot to receive the pass back from Point and direct the puck through the legs of Varlamov.

"That was a special play," Point said. "I don't think many guys would think to do that. Just a great play. He's a guy that's so good with the puck, he knows what he's doing with it. That was something I don't think I've seen before but it was super nice."

For Point that's about as gushing of a comment as you will hear him make. But even as he was trying to put that description into words, Gourde was sitting next to him with a bit of a sly smirk on his face while slightly nodding his head, clearly agreeing with Point's assessment.

Kucherov made it seem like a run of the mill play he just happened to pull out of his arsenal at the right moment to execute the pass.

"I saw [Shattenkirk] making the long pass and I didn't know if the D's going to step up on me or not so I just try to chip over his stick and get it over to Pointer," Kucherov said.

It even overshadowed the opening goal of the game by Point, who made a stutter-step power move around Ryan Pulock to get to the net and score his first of the night 74 seconds into the game that set the tone. He followed that up with a power play goal as he set up at the right post, raised his stick to silently call for the puck and then knocked a Victor Hedman pass out of the air just above ankle level for his second of the night.

As brilliant of a display that was put on in Game 1, it was just one game and the Lightning had plenty go their way. Game 2 is a chance for the Islanders to reset and Tampa Bay to regroup.

"Still think there's parts of our game that we can be better at," Hedman said. "You can look at everything but at the end of the day it's one game and for us, we're obviously happy with scoring eight goals. That's not what you're gonna expect going into games but you know we have the skill and we had the looks to score those goals but we obviously expect them to bring it next game but we also expect ourselves to raise our game to another level." ■

Brayden Point scores during the first period. Point lived up to his last name with two goals and three assists in Tampa Bay's dominant Game 1 victory.

SEPTEMBER 9, 2020 · EDMONTON, ALBERTA
LIGHTNING 2, ISLANDERS 1

UNFORGETTABLE FINISH

Kucherov Goal in Final Seconds Gives Lightning Emotional Win

Hockey is filled with heart.

To excel at the highest level, players put every bit of that heart into their play. It's why there is so much emotion in the game. It's why there are fights and rapid reactions and anger and, sometimes, rage.

But it's also why there are leaping celebrations, hugs and helmet taps.

That's just in the regular season.

Pour all that into a playoff mixer and that emotion comes bursting out of the blender, just as it did with under nine seconds remaining on the clock when Nikita Kucherov scored to give the Tampa Bay Lightning a 2-1 victory in Game 2 of the Eastern Conference finals.

So many elements of the game were working against the Lightning: from allowing an early goal and losing a forward to ejection six minutes into the game to losing Brayden Point to injury in the second period, which forced Tampa Bay to finish the game with nine forwards.

"It was one of those games that we were kind of fighting the circumstances of the game," forward Blake Coleman said. "There was just a lot of kills, not many guys on the bench up front. Those are the games that feel the best and obviously it all came out there at the end...we were fired up."

In the first period it was a five-minute penalty kill was the result of a major for boarding on Alex Killorn following a hit to Brock Nelson. With it a 1-1 game deep into the third period, Tampa Bay stared down a 5-on-3 penalty kill for 38 seconds with 10 minutes left in the third period.

"We kill off a five-minute major early in the game and then we get, for whatever reason, basically another five minute major in the sense we got two back-to-back penalties and had to kill off a five-on-three," Lightning head coach Jon Cooper said. "So when you get to the point we were at...there's so many things that happen on the way to what how this game ended."

That emotional outburst came from an exhilarating final push in the closing seconds.

It started with Yanni Gourde racing in on a partial breakaway off a perfect pass from Ondrej Palat. Gourde was denied on his backhand chance

Victor Hedman celebrates with teammates after scoring in the first period to tie Game 2, 1-1.

as Semyon Varlamov steered the puck to the end boards. Gourde was able to retrieve the loose puck and reverse it for Nikita Kucherov trailing behind.

As Kucherov drew the attention of the entire New York defense – a rare situation for the Islanders who had all five players inside the right circle – Palat slipped in all alone at the top of the crease where Kucherov found him for a wide open chance that he put just wide of the net.

Andy Greene recovered the puck and curled back behind the net and tried to rim the puck around the boards, but Gourde was able to disrupt the play enough to slow the puck down. Ryan McDonagh, pinching down on the weak side, was able to collect the puck along the boards at the hash marks, just before he gave a look over toward the net where he spotted Kucherov.

McDonagh then whipped a pass past three Islanders defenders as Kucherov peered around the bodies to find the puck and shimmied back just enough to get his stick in position to whip a one-timer past Varlamov with 8.8 seconds left on the clock and spark an emotional outburst from any player donning blue or on the bench behind players in blue.

"We just kind of had a little bit of pressure going and I knew there wasn't much time left," McDonagh said. "So I just tried to stay a little bit deeper at that end and just try to make sure I got the puck clean off the wall. I made a little eye contact with Kuch there and was just hoping he was going to stay a little bit close to the back post. So I'm just trying to put it where he can get the puck to the net and Kuch did a great job finishing it off. A huge, huge win no doubt."

That set off the emotions.

Kucherov quickly skated back in the direction of the blue line, dropped to a knee and let out a primal scream. He got back on his skates and met Palat and Goodrow with a quick leaping hug, then quickly turned around to embrace Mikhail Sergachev and McDonagh.

On the bench, Cooper let out three giant fist pumps in celebration avoiding contact with assistant coach Derrick Lalonde. The remaining players on the bench began exchanging hugs, not even noticing Cooper behind them.

"I missed it, I guess I was busy hugging I think every guy on the bench," Coleman said.

It was one of those type of moments that the individual play of the parts equaled to something greater than the whole. That's how all the emotion came pouring out.

They are raw, they are real, they are tangible and on display for everybody to see.

"That's why you play the game," McDonagh said. "As a team all that hard work and preparation from the coaching staff down to the players, we're all working towards the same goal here, the ultimate goal. A dramatic finish like that, it's one moment to be a part of a group that wants to continue those great moments here and continue to gain confidence. In whatever situation, whatever scenario, if the games are tight, down in the game or up in the game there's no quit in our group. We got a lot of gutsy players and it's fun to want to be a part of." ■

Lightning and Islanders players tangle during the first period of Game 2. Tampa Bay's Alex Killorn was assessed a major for boarding following a hit to New York's Brock Nelson.

SEPTEMBER 11, 2020 · EDMONTON, ALBERTA
ISLANDERS 5, LIGHTNING 3

"OUR OWN WORST ENEMY"

Late Lightning Penalties, Missed Opportunities Lead to Loss

In the pre-COVID hockey season, the Tampa Bay Lightning had four players reach the 20-goal mark before the world hit the pause button.

In Game 3 of the Eastern Conference finals, the Lightning were missing three of those players with Alex Killorn suspended, Brayden Point injured and Steven Stamkos still not healthy. Yet, Tampa Bay put together a strong enough effort to grab a stranglehold on the series. If not for the most dangerous opponent the Lightning tend to face, things could have finished differently and the tone of the series would have been much, much different.

But Tampa Bay ran into the Lightning, and, well, that was the biggest reason for the 5-3 loss.

Brock Nelson's goal with 3:25 left in the third period broke a tie, coming directly off a rare Ryan McDonagh mistake, thwarting the Lightning's third-period rally from down two goals.

The goal occurred after McDonagh tried to go up the middle to Barclay Goodrow, who was blanketed by Nelson and allowed the puck to stay in the Tampa Bay zone. Anthony Beauvillier's shot attempt was blocked but the puck squirted back to the Islanders forward who then swung a pass to Nelson at the bottom of the right circle.

One game after making the play to set up Nikita Kucherov for the winner in the final seconds, McDonagh wound up on the opposite side for New York's winner in the final minutes of Game 3.

"We were our own worst enemy," Lightning head coach Jon Cooper said. "When you get to this stage and you're playing elite teams like the Islanders are, you can't give them chances or extra chances. And we hand delivered a couple to them and good teams will make you pay. They did tonight."

Tampa Bay was done in by mistakes that, for the most part, they have been able to avoid throughout the playoffs.

Such as the McDonagh play. Or Mitchell Stephens failing to get enough on a clearing attempt that kept the puck in the zone and led to Adam Pelech's go-ahead goal at 11:50 of the second period. Or McDonagh failing to pick up Anthony Beauvillier in front of the net on a switch-off that made it 3-1 two minutes after Pelech scored.

It was one of those sags that lasted about five minutes for Tampa Bay, the kind of lost focus that during the regular season you chalk up and move on. From the moment Stephens was called for slashing until the Beauvillier goal the Lightning were out attempted by a 7-1 margin in the span of 4:44.

"That's what happens," Cooper said. "We've got a game plan and if you're going to turn some pucks over and take penalties you're going to put yourself in a tough spot. We avoided both those mistakes in game one and two and if we did make them, we got away

Lightning goalie Andrei Vasilevskiy and teammates Anthony Cirelli (71) and Ryan McDonagh (27) show their frustration following an Islanders goal in the second period.

with them. We didn't get away with them tonight so sometimes these are lessons learned."

Despite those mistakes the Lightning were in the game for the most part. In each period, the Lightning held the advantage in possession at 5-on-5 play.

Down by two entering the third, Ondrej Palat tapped in a Kucherov pass for a power play goal 2:32 into the final period to cut the deficit to one. Tyler Johnson would tie the game with 7:56 left in

regulation, deflecting down a point shot from Erik Cernak to get the game back on even standing with his first goal since Game 5 against Columbus.

"It's on us, they didn't do anything we didn't know was coming or put us under pressure," Cooper said. "We just made some bad decisions." ∎

SEPTEMBER 13, 2020 · EDMONTON, ALBERTA
LIGHTNING 4, ISLANDERS 1

LIGHTNING-FAST REVERSAL

Coleman, Palat Goals 12 Seconds Apart Lead Tampa Bay to Game 4 Win

Twenty-seven seconds.

That's how long it took for Tampa Bay's lightning quick attack to completely reverse fortune against the New York Islanders in Game 4 of the Eastern Conference finals and fuel the Lightning to a 4-1 victory. Tampa Bay leads the series 3-1 and is on the verge of clinching a berth in the Stanley Cup Final for the third time in franchise history.

Twenty-seven seconds after the Lightning fell behind, Tampa Bay had the lead. In real time, it took just over two minutes to crush the Islanders' spirits for the second time in the series.

Goals by Blake Coleman and Ondrej Palat 12 seconds apart, the fastest two goals scored by the Lightning in franchise history, quickly turned a 1-0 deficit into a 2-1 lead.

Coleman's goal came 15 seconds after Brock Nelson put New York in front, partly due to a coverage breakdown by Coleman, who started to leave the defensive zone too quickly, allowing Nelson to get around him and gain the open space in the high slot to rip off a wrist shot past Andrei Vasilevskiy at 11:27 of the second period.

Lightning head coach Jon Cooper did not hesitate to put Coleman and his line right back out on the ice.

"I'm not a big believer in just because you got scored on you go to the bench and think about it," Cooper said. "Get out there and get it back. Now I can't sit here and say I thought they'd get it back in 15 seconds or whatever it was but it's a game, it's not a shift and those guys have a job to do. I want them to go do it and part of my job is to make sure they've got the confidence going to do their job. I have full confidence in them and in they delivered."

The goal came after New York won a faceoff at center ice and quickly dumped the puck into the Tampa Bay zone.

Vasilevskiy collected the puck behind the net and with no forecheck coming in on him, had the time to find Yanni Gourde in the corner. Gourde caught Coleman set to take off from his own blue line and put a puck high into the air down the ice.

"I looked up I kind of see (Coleman) in full stride,"

New York's Leo Komarov crashes into Tampa Bay goaltender Andrei Vasilevskiy during the first period of Game 4.

Gourde said. "So I kind of threw the puck to an area where I think he can beat his guy. Obviously, it worked out perfectly and he beat his guy and was able to get the puck and score that goal."

Coleman was able to settle the puck and get enough of a handle on it to elude a poke check by Semyon Varlamov, pull the puck to his backhand and tuck it in the net to tie the game.

"Obviously as a player that prides myself, and our line as well, just on being two-way guys and reliable guys, getting scored on doesn't sit really well," Coleman said. "But credit to Coop keeping us out there and give us a shot to go get it back. It was a good response...and it's big anytime you can respond quickly in a game, it's going to swing the momentum right back.

"Then our big boys took over from there."

The big boys are the Lightning's top line with Nikita Kucherov, Ondrej Palat and Brayden Point, the line that went out to take the next shift after Coleman's goal.

And before the Islanders could collect themselves from giving up the lead so quickly, the Lightning struck again.

Off the next faceoff, all five players touched the puck as Point won it back to Kevin Shattenkirk and 12 seconds later, Palat put Tampa Bay in front.

Kucherov circled back to take a pass from Ryan McDonagh and as he gained the blue line, Kucherov gave the puck over to Point to his right. Point gave it back to Kucherov, drawing both New York defenseman to him, leaving the path down the left-wing side wide open for Palat.

With a quick backhand pass, Kucherov was able to find Palat for wrist shot that went in off the blocker of Varalmov after hitting the inside of the post.

"We're confident in our group" Palat said. "We have a ton of depth in this organization that we trust so we have confidence in every single one of us and I think it's a big part of the game."

The return of Point proved a big factor for the Lightning as well. After missing Game 3, his presence provided a spark even as he missed the final 9:37 of the game after a hit in the corner that appeared to aggravate whatever might be ailing him. He did remain on the bench for the remainder of the game, but not before putting his final stamp on the game.

Point found Kucherov to gain the zone and, because Kucherov drew the attention of the Islanders once again as Pelech tried to step up at the right circle, Kucherov was able to find Palat at the left circle that created a mini two-on-one chance and Palat was able to wait out Pulock and slip a backhand pass over to Point in the crease for a 3-1 lead 3:33 into the third period.

"We were trying to manage him and he was all over it, he was in on everything and setting up goals, scoring goals and he's a big part of our team," Cooper said of Point. "But we have to manage him. It's the playoffs and these guys are playing hard, hard minutes and then you watch the intensity in these games and they just keep increasing with every game that's played in every round that's played." ∎

Brayden Point celebrates after scoring a goal in the third period of Tampa Bay's 4-1 win in Game 4.

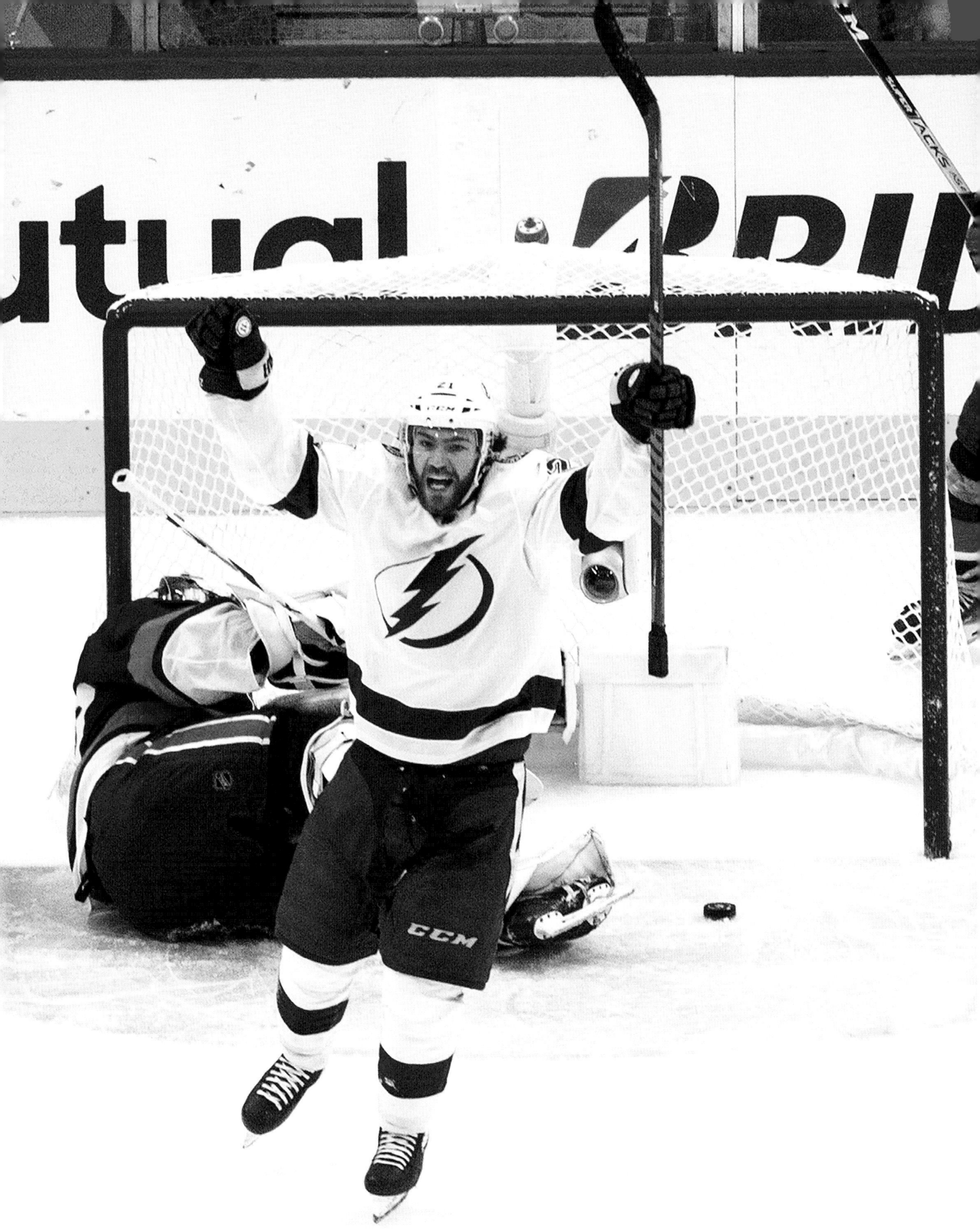
CCM

SEPTEMBER 15, 2020 · EDMONTON, ALBERTA
ISLANDERS 2, LIGHTNING 1 (2OT)

RAZOR THIN

Islanders Take Closely Fought Game 5 in Second Overtime

There are a million reasons to fall in love with the game of hockey.

Game 5 of the Eastern Conference finals was not one of them, especially for fans of the Tampa Bay Lightning.

Because for more than 90 minutes a team can remain disciplined, structured and play great defensive hockey only to see an unfortunate break deny the opportunity to advance to the Stanley Cup Final.

The game, even in its beauty, can be downright ugly.

For the Lightning, that's exactly what it looked like in a game that had very little action even while providing so much drama.

Jordan Eberle scored on a 2-on-1 chance from a pass by Anders Lee at 12:30 of the second overtime to give the New York Islanders a 2-1 victory in Game of the Eastern Conference finals to force a Game 6.

The Lightning did more than enough to win this game despite the absence of No. 1 center Brayden Point for the second time in the series. And they did more right – way more – than they did wrong. But sometimes in this crazy, beautiful game, you still lose.

The game-winning goal, which came 92 minutes, 30 seconds into the game, was the 24th shot on goal of the game for the Islanders. The 24th.

This game was more of a product of the way Tampa Bay has played throughout these playoffs combined with the style of play New York institutes. It was a game of blocked shots, limited opportunities and waiting for the other to blink.

And when that opportunity arose for the Islanders, they took advantage when Kevin Shattenkirk scuffed a shot attempt from the right point that led to the odd-man rush.

"Winning and losing is razor thin in this league," Lightning head coach Jon Cooper said. "It took the stars aligning on a fanned shot for them to get the break they got and they still had to take advantage of it and they did. So that's what happens in this game. We had opportunities to put the game away and either a bounce here or save there, a block shot here... but if you look at the game as a whole, if we keep doing that we're pretty confident in our group in a seven-game series."

Through regulation time, New York was held to 16 shots on goal and 20 through four periods.

It was as strong of a defensive effort as the Lightning have put forth in the playoffs to date.

"We kept them to the outside most of the night, I thought," defenseman Victor Hedman said. "For us it's overall the whole game we were pretty much in their end."

It can also be a game of inches in these type of close game.

Islanders goaltender Semyon Varlamov deflects an Ondrej Palat shot in overtime. New York ultimately took Game 5 on a Jordan Eberle goal in the second overtime.

Late in the second period Tampa Bay had a 5-on-3 rush up the ice. Carter Verhaeghe would find Zach Bogosian as the trailer at the right circle but with the top part of the net open, Bogosian hit the post.

"Carter made a nice seam pass to me," Bogosian said. "I saw an opening and just tried to jump in the hole and unfortunately it hit the post."

It was also about some wasted chances as Tampa Bay had a four-minute power play with 1:23 left, but generated only two shots on goal as the power play carried over to the start of the first overtime.

In the end, however, the way Tampa Bay played is a model for how they want to play maintaining the belief it will lead to a positive result more often than not.

"We believe in what we're doing," Cooper said. "We didn't come into these playoffs thinking we were going to go 16-0 at all. We just came into these playoffs with the mindset we're going to win 16 games. The way you have to win those games is defend the way we've been defending. We keep doing that, I have a lot of faith in this group." ∎

SEPTEMBER 17, 2020 · EDMONTON, ALBERTA
LIGHTNING 2, ISLANDERS 1 (OT)

A NEW CHAPTER

Cirelli OT Goal Returns Lightning to Stanley Cup Final

When the Tampa Bay Lightning entered training camp in September of 2019, they wanted to a new story with a better ending.

The previous one provided an ending that made them want to rip the pages out one-by-one and send them into the shredder.

Now the Lightning have the opportunity to not only finish this rewrite on the right page, they have the chance to use the shredded paper for a ticket-tape parade, provided they can even hold one.

Anthony Cirelli's goal at 13:18 of overtime finished off the latest chapter to give Tampa Bay a 2-1 victory against the New York Islanders in Game 6 of the Eastern Conference finals and send the Lightning to the Stanley Cup Final for the third time in franchise history and a date against the Dallas Stars.

It's already been a story unlike any other, with one final chapter still to be written.

History cannot be erased and Tampa Bay has never tried to hide from what happened at the end of the 2018-19 season in a four-game sweep at the hands of the Columbus Blue Jackets. But what the Lightning set out to accomplish at the start of this season – which began at the opening of training camp on Sept. 12, 2019 – was to write a new story.

And to this point, it's been all about redemption that started with a first-round series, five-game victory against the Columbus Blue Jackets followed by a five-game series victory against division rival Boston. And finally, the six-game victory over the New York Islanders and head coach Barry Trotz, who was behind the bench for the Washington Capitals the last time Tampa Bay was in the Eastern Conference finals and failed to advance after holding a 3-2 series lead.

That's only part of the redemption story the Lightning are trying to write. The meatiest chapters center around the way Tampa Bay approaches the way they play. Not stylistically nor system wise, but in a more patient and mindful approach. Attack the game with a different mindset by not beating themselves.

It requires the type of patience the Lightning have not been able to maintain in previous years.

Anthony Cirelli scores in overtime to win Game 6 and send the Lightning to the Stanley Cup Final.

It has paid off as Tampa Bay is the first team in NHL history to win each of their first three series with the clinching victory in overtime, have played two overtime games in each series, winning five of them including the five-overtime thriller to open the playoffs in the first round against Columbus.

No team in NHL history has played more overtime minutes in a playoff season than the 2020 Lightning.

And just like the playoff season to date, the Conference finals clinching game was a test of that patience in a game that Tampa Bay finished with a 103-64 advantage in shot attempts.

And yet, the score was 1-1 through 60 minute of regulation time before heading to overtime.

"It wears on you, there's no doubt," Lightning head coach Jon Cooper said. "That's where you look at a little bit of the mental makeup and a little bit of our maturity because we felt halfway through that game we could have been up a lot more than a tie game. They were defending and their goalie was obviously playing extremely well so you know when you're bending a little bit at parts of the game we did, that's where you're thinking, 'Hey we deserve to be in a better spot than we are being tied,' but the guys they hung in there and they stuck with it."

Things could have went sideways for the Lightning after only being able to show a tie score for the strong effort they put in, even going back to Game 5, which played out very similarly to how Game 6 was going. Right down to the four-minute power play the Lightning received at the end of regulation for high sticking call on the Islanders. Just like Game 5, Tampa Bay failed to convert on the opportunity that carried over to the extra period with the clean sheet of ice, even giving up a shorthanded breakaway to Brock Nelson that was stopped by Andrei Vasilevskiy.

But just as the Lightning are looking to do with these playoffs, Tampa Bay wrote a different ending this time around with the heroics coming from a player who has made a habit of coming through in big moments.

With Tampa Bay on a line change, Cirelli remained out and headed right to the forecheck alone with four Islanders players in the defensive zone. Going in on a 1-on-2 situation, Cirelli won the puck and turned toward the boards. That allowed enough time for Barclay Goodrow to come in with support and take a pass from Cirelli to carry puck below the goal line.

Cirelli, at the end of his shift, headed to the net and stopped just on top of the crease. Goodrow cut back behind the net and fed a pass to Cirelli, who shoveled it in off the far post before it trickled along the goal line eventually settling down just behind the line and send the Lightning to the Cup Final.

In his playing career, Cirelli also had the overtime goal to win the Memorial Cup with Oshawa in 2015 and scored the overtime winner for Erie in 2017 for the Ontario Hockey League championship.

This was his first career NHL overtime goal.

"The kid has scored big goals in his career," Cooper said. "And we truly believe when you play the right way good things are going to happen and that's what that kid does."

It's another chapter in a story the Lightning hope finishes with a happy ending.

"The emotions are so high," Cirelli said. "We worked all year. Our goal is to be playing for the Stanley Cup. We're here now. I think it's every kid's dream to be in this situation." ∎

Lightning teammates swarm Anthony Cirelli after scoring the game-winning goal in overtime.